Studies in Musical Genesis and Structure

General Editor: Lewis Lockwood, Harvard University

Studies in Musical Genesis and Structure

Anna Bolena and the Artistic Maturity of Gaetano Donizetti
Philip Gossett

Beethoven's Diabelli Variations

WILLIAM KINDERMAN

CLARENDON PRESS · OXFORD
1987

Oxford University Press, Walton Street, Oxford OX2 6DP
Oxford New York Toronto
Delhi Bombay Calcutta Madras Karachi
Petaling Jaya Singapore Hong Kong Tokyo
Nairobi Dar es Salaam Cape Town
Melbourne Auckland

and associated companies in
Beirut Berlin Ibadan Nicosia

Oxford is a trade mark of Oxford University Press

Published in the United States
by Oxford University Press, New York

British Library Cataloguing in Publication Data
Kinderman, William
Beethoven's Diabelli variations.—
(Studies in musical genesis and structure)
1. Beethoven, Ludwig van. Selections
(Sketches)
I. Title II. Series
780'.92'4   ML410.B4
ISBN 0-19-315323-8

Library of Congress Cataloging in Publication Data
Kinderman, William.
Beethoven's Diabelli variations.
(Studies in musical genesis and structure)
Bibliography: p.
Includes index.
1. Beethoven, Ludwig van, 1170–1827.   Veränderungen
über einen Walzer.   I. Title.   II. Series.
MT145.B4K56   1987   786.1'092'4   86-8590
ISBN 0-19-315323-8

Typeset by Joshua Associates Limited, Oxford
Printed in Great Britain
at the Alden Press, Oxford

to
Professor Dieter Weber

in memoriam

Contents

Editor's Preface

HISTORICAL musicology has recently witnessed vigorous and wide-ranging efforts to deepen understanding of the compositional procedures by which composers of various periods and traditions brought their works to realization. In part this trend has resulted from renewed and intensive study of the manuscript sources of works by many of the major figures in Western music history, especially those for whom new and authoritative editions of their complete works are being undertaken. In part it has arisen from the desire to establish more cogent and precise claims about the formative backgrounds of individual works than could be accomplished by more general stylistic study. In many cases, the fortunate survival of much of the composer's working materials—his sketches, drafts, composing scores, corrected copies, and the like—has stimulated this approach on a scale that could not have been dreamed of a century ago, when Gustav Nottebohm's pioneering studies of Beethoven's sketches and drafts first appeared.

Accordingly, this series aims to provide a number of short monographs, each dealing with an individual work by an important composer. The main focus will be on the genesis of the work from its known antecedent stages to its final realization, so far as these can be determined from the known sources; and in each case a view of the genesis of the work will be connected to an analytical overview of the finished composition. Every monograph will be written by a specialist, and, apart from the general theme, no artificial uniformity will be imposed. The individual character of both the work and the evidence, as well as the special viewpoint of the author, will inevitably dictate certain differences in emphasis and treatment. Thus some of these studies may stress the combination of sketch evidence and analysis, while others may place stronger emphasis on the position of the work within the conventions of its genre. Although no such series could possibly aim at being comprehensive, my hope is that it will deal with a representative number and variety of works by composers of stature, including Bach, Mozart, Beethoven, Brahms, Wagner, Richard Strauss, Schoenberg, and Berg.

William Kinderman's study of the compositional origins of Beethoven's Diabelli Variations, Op. 120, is the first extended investigation of the sketches for this work. In contrast to earlier views of its chronology, Kinderman shows that it was begun in 1819, then put aside for several years, and then resumed and completed in 1822-3. His exploration of the sketches for individual segments of the cycle, and his view of the cycle in the context of Beethoven's works of these years, illuminates the special place of the Diabelli Variations among the monumental achievements of Beethoven's last period.

Harvard University   Lewis Lockwood

Acknowledgements

In the course of this study, I have become indebted to an international community of scholars. For helpful advice and criticism from the earliest stages, I am grateful to Alan Tyson, Andrew Imbrie, Kevin Korsyn, and especially to Robert Winter, who generously showed me some of his then unpublished material on Beethoven's late sketches. Daniel Heartz kindly lent me transcriptions of Beethoven's sketches for the Diabelli Variations made by the late Erich Hertzmann, now in his possession. Martin Staehelin, former Director of the Beethoven-Archiv in Bonn, generously allowed me access to materials in this rich collection and provided me with excellent working conditions in Bonn.

I am grateful to the Deutscher Akademischer Austauschdienst, the University of California at Berkeley, the University of Victoria, and the Social Sciences and Humanities Research Council of Canada for financial support that enabled me to examine Beethoven's original manuscripts in Germany and France. I am also grateful to the following institutions for their helpful assistance in allowing me access to Beethoven's manuscripts: Bibliothèque Nationale, Paris; Staatsbibliothek preussischer Kulturbesitz, West Berlin; Deutsche Staatsbibliothek, East Berlin; Musée Ingres, Montauban, France.

My profoundest gratitude is to Joseph Kerman, Sieghard Brandenburg, and Lewis Lockwood, each of whom read the entire manuscript and made many valuable and detailed suggestions.

Portions of this book have appeared in different form in the *Journal of the American Musicological Society* and in *Zu Beethoven: Aufsätze und Dokumente*, in German translation. I am grateful to the editors of these publications for their permission to republish these materials. I am also grateful to Rosemary Smith for preparing the music examples, and to Bruce Phillips and Carol Cumming of Oxford University Press for their assistance in seeing the book through to publication. Financial support for preparation of the music examples was provided by the University of Victoria. This book has been published with the help of a grant from the Canadian Federation for the Humanities, using funds provided by the Social Sciences and Humanities Research Council of Canada.

To my wife, Eva, I owe a special debt of thanks. Her comprehensive knowledge of Beethoven's piano works contributed substantially to this study. At the same time, she defended my quiet, and enabled me to work, sometimes under difficult circumstances.

This book is dedicated to the memory of my deceased teacher and friend Dieter Weber, professor of piano at the Hochschule für Musik in Vienna until his tragic premature death ten years ago, in February 1976. My wife and I were privileged to study with Weber as part of his international class of selected students. Few who knew him remained uninfluenced by his profound intellect and his uncompromisingly high standards of performance. My original interest in the Diabelli Variations arose from performances of the work by John O'Conor, who was then a student in Weber's class. The ultimate outcome of my study, on the other hand, goes beyond the present book in the form of my own performance of the Variations, which I have played widely in North America and Europe, and intend to record.

December 1986   W.K.

List of Illustrations
(*between pp. 12 and 13*)

Introduction

THE *Thirty-three Variations on a Waltz by Diabelli*, Op. 120, represent Beethoven's most extraordinary single achievement in the art of variation-writing, and in their originality and power of invention stand beside other late masterpieces such as the Ninth Symphony, the *Missa Solemnis*, and the last quartets. When Anton Diabelli announced the publication of this work in 1823, he proclaimed these Variations 'a great and important masterpiece worthy to be ranked with the imperishable creations of the Classics', entitled 'to a place beside Sebastian Bach's masterpiece in the same form',[1] the Goldberg Variations. This is still the general critical verdict. Nevertheless, as in the case of other late works by Beethoven, the difficulty, great length, and complexity of the Diabelli Variations have conspired against frequent performances, and have posed as obstacles to satisfactory comprehension of the work as a whole. Paradox lies at the heart of this composition—Beethoven's sublime transformations of a theme he disdained as a 'cobbler's patch'[2]—and its psychological complexity as well as its huge dimensions seem to stand in the way of lucid appreciation.

It is therefore fortunate that we possess a source of information and elucidation for the Variations which derives its authority from the composer himself—Beethoven's own sketches and drafts for the work. From these documents we can discern the true chronological sequence for the composition of Op. 120, various stages in its genesis, and aspects of Beethoven's compositional process. Moreover, these preliminary documents point towards important aspects of the finished composition that have been overlooked by the numerous commentators who have written about the Variations. As these sources show, the revelation of Beethoven's compositional process can enhance our understanding of the music by providing a key to the unique internal context that lies behind the work as we know it.

In the present study of the Diabelli Variations, therefore, I have utilized Beethoven's sketches and drafts as the initial focus of my investigation,

---

[1] Cited in Donald Francis Tovey, *Essays in Musical Analysis: Chamber Music* (London, 1944), p. 124. The original German text is given in Alexander Wheelock Thayer, *Chronologisches Verzeichniss der Werke Ludwig van Beethovens* (Berlin, 1865), p. 151.

[2] Beethoven's initial distaste for the waltz is reported by Anton Schindler. See Schindler, *Beethoven As I Knew Him*, trans. Constance S. Jolly, ed. Donald MacArdle (London and Chapel Hill, 1966), p. 252.

coupled with an analytical discussion of the completed work, drawing upon insights gained from the sketches. A primary concern of my study is the finished piece apart from the sketches, and although, in principle at least, there are few points in the analytical part of this book which could not have been made independently of a knowledge of Beethoven's compositional process, in fact, the outlook presented here is considerably different from any that has hitherto been advanced, and is in crucial ways indebted to Beethoven's sketches. Expressed metaphorically, it is as if this revelation of the genesis of the work represented a ladder to be thrown away once we have climbed up it. My analytical discussion must stand or fall on aesthetic grounds, and should not require any special pleading derived from the intricacies of Beethoven's sketches.

Nevertheless, I should not like to throw away the ladder. As a human act and the outcome of a creative process, Beethoven's composition is a product of decisions much more richly documented in the sketches than in the finished piece. Nor is it true, as is sometimes claimed, that the sketches reveal only negative decisions of the composer—material later changed or omitted— since they also highlight the subsequent positive decisions embodied in the completed work. By uncovering the context of conceptual and intuitive acts whose products now stand as passages in the art work, the sketches can deepen our perception of the work. The challenge in interpreting them consists of bringing sufficient insight to bear on the composer's creative process so that we can discern clearly his musical intention.

To deal with the artist's 'intention' is of course to enter treacherous territory. But as Philip Gossett once pointed out, the 'intentional fallacy', as formulated in literary criticism, is not applicable to the study of musical sketches, for their subject is the materials of the art work.[3] Record of the creative evolution of these materials indeed provides evidence of artistic 'intention' by the documentation of compositional decisions. On the other hand, it is well to remember that sketches are private documents, and by their very nature provisional. Investigations into musical sketches must be entered cautiously, or there is danger of over-interpretation of a fragile network of evidence. But where all the evidence in unequivocal, there is nothing to prevent disclosure of the composer's intention. In such cases the relevance to analysis of musical sketches is obvious: they can function as a guide to critical investigation, and even as a corrective for analysis gone astray. By casting illumination on Beethoven's compositional ideas and attitudes, the sketches may help to show us which internal relationships in a piece are genuinely significant, and which are merely coincidental or accidental.

The most articulate recent spokesman on behalf of the analytic relevance of sketch studies, Sieghard Brandenburg, has marshalled these and other

[3] Gossett, 'Beethoven's Sixth Symphony: Sketches for the First Movement', *Journal of the American Musicological Society*, xxvii (1974), pp. 260-1.

arguments in support of a view in which biographical and analytical concerns are regarded as interdependent aspects of critical evaluation.[4] Brandenburg observes on the one hand that analysis is inevitably founded in categories indebted to an historical context, and on the other, that the biographical realm of the sketches provides material for analysis inasmuch as it clarifies the composer's musical intention. This position has much to recommend it, not the least of which is its refusal to abide a facile distinction between 'biography' and 'analysis'. And while some analysts may hesitate to embrace Brandenburg's position out of excessive devotion to the notion of the 'work itself', lifted out of its historical context, few will disdain the import of the sketches when it can be shown that they lead us towards significant musical insights. That this is sometimes the case can be no better illustrated than by Beethoven's sketches for the Diabelli Variations.

In particular, the major revelation of the sketches and drafts for Op. 120—that Beethoven had conceived two-thirds of the variations, down to the penultimate fugue, in 1819, and then set the work aside for several years before finishing it in 1823—is of considerable importance when we study the completed work. This sheds much light on those variations composed later and on the form of the whole, and clarifies Beethoven's unique solution to the artistic problems that faced him in this immense set of variations. This composition reflects the history of its genesis, and the record of Beethoven's creative process is all the more significant here because of its divided chronology in composition.

This information surely would have interested any of the numerous analysts who have already grappled with Op. 120, none of whose studies are wholly satisfactory. Some are outrageously unsatisfactory. Karl Geiringer and Michel Butor, for example, have both tried to find a structural plan similar to that of Bach's Goldberg Variations in Beethoven's work.[5] According to this scheme, the form of the whole is perfectly symmetrical, made up of groups of four or eight variations with the paired march variations (Nos. 16–17) acting as a centrepiece. This plan neglects many audible facts of the piece, some of which were pointed out by David Porter in a response to Geiringer's article.[6] But had these critics been familiar with the genesis of the Variations, it is doubtful that they could have proposed such a plan in the first place. When Beethoven expanded his draft of the whole work in 1822–3, he left his older variation order internally intact for the most part, but opened with two new variations (the present Vars. 1 and 2), added many more variations towards the

---

[4] See Brandenburg's discussion in *19th-Century Music*, ii (1979), pp. 270–4.

[5] See Butor, *Dialogue avec 33 variations de Ludwig van Beethoven sur une valse de Diabelli* (Paris, 1971), pp. 33–8; Geiringer, 'The Structure of Beethoven's Diabelli Variations', *Musical Quarterly*, l (1964), pp. 496–503.

[6] Porter, 'The Structure of Beethoven's Diabelli Variations, Op. 120', *Music Review*, xxxi (1970), pp. 295–7.

end, and inserted one at the middle of the set. As we shall see, these added variations contribute substantially to the form of the whole work, imposing not a symmetrical but an asymmetrical plan, an overall progression culminating in the last five variations. The work as we know it is thus to a great extent the product of two superimposed conceptions. The presence of a totally symmetrical plan analogous to the Goldberg Variations is unthinkable—even if it had been evident in the previous order, it would have been completely disrupted when Beethoven finished the piece.

On the other hand, the inserted variations added by Beethoven in 1823 contribute a subtle dimension to the set whose implications transcend the purely musical sphere. Most of them are, in one sense or another, parodistic variations, and while this is clear enough on close inspection, it is sufficiently subtle to have been overlooked by previous commentators. This issue of parody in Op. 120 is complex, and we shall have occasion later to explore it in considerable detail. It is interesting that in Op. 120, the overall formal progression of the Variations relies heavily on parody of the melody of Diabelli's theme, an idea which, though prominent in the finished piece, is not in evidence in the 1819 Draft. A sense of the unity of the whole work, such as we find in other works of the composer, is present in Op. 120, but here, since the variations are based on a trivial theme not of the composer's making, the whole spans a tension from ironic caricature to sublime transformation of the waltz of Diabelli. This extra-musical dimension of parody is essential to a full understanding of the piece, although by its very nature it is not immediately obvious in the 'work itself', especially, perhaps, to ears conditioned by the narrowly formalistic bias prevalent in some recent music scholarship. In both the positive sense as a guide for analysis, and the negative sense as a corrective for analysis, therefore, the sketches for Op. 120 provide a sound justification for the position articulated by Brandenburg.

The notion of the 'work itself' is indispensable inasmuch as it allows us to assess internal coherence of a piece on terms implicit in the music, but it is a nuisance if it serves as an excuse to ignore other relevant factors, be they historical, sociological, or, in this case, biographical. In reality, works of art cannot be wholly divorced from these parameters; nor is it desirable that they should be. The great achievement of music scholarship based on primary sources—on Bach a generation ago, and more recently on Beethoven—has been to restore a pragmatic, human sense of their extraordinary accomplishments. If we are now to address Beethoven's music in its proper aesthetic terms, it is well not to enlist new studies of sources with a too narrowly limited concept of analysis intent upon non-valuational precision modelled on the methods of the natural sciences, but with the humanistic tradition of criticism. All of the most rigorous methods of analysis can be employed critically if they serve not as an end in themselves but as a means to an end: the elucidation of the most significant and meaningful aspects of works of art.

And with the co-ordination of analysis with criticism we can also symbolize a willingness to assimilate whatever historical and psychological phenomena prove relevant in a given musical work.

The present study is a critical examination of the Diabelli Variations and its genesis. Part I includes a reconstruction of Beethoven's sketches for Op. 120, documents which have not before been viewed clearly because of their thorough physical dismemberment. I have not attempted exhaustive description of the sketches but rather have tried to cull the most salient relationships which arise in them. (The reader is invited to consult the transcriptions in Part III and to discover additional points.) I have attempted, on the other hand, to supply a complete chronological history of the genesis of Op. 120, insomuch as this is possible. I have also endeavoured to project a sense of the vitality and spontaneous creativity of the material in these sources, especially in the Wittgenstein Sketchbook, which is the most interesting from the standpoint of Beethoven's creative process. It will be evident that I do not agree with Gustav Nottebohm's dictum that 'the spirit that dictates the work does not appear in the sketches'.[7] The marks of creativity certainly do manifest themselves in these pages.

In the second part of this study I have attempted comprehensive treatment of the work as we know it, drawing upon insights gained from Beethoven's sketches and drafts. The complex problem of parody calls for a separate discussion, as does Beethoven's interpretation of Diabelli's waltz. The variations are discussed, not in an exhaustive analysis, but in an attempt to characterize what is most striking and singular in each of them. The nature of their succession and of the large form that embraces the whole emerges from the cumulative effect of the individual variations and can be properly expressed only through examination of the entire massive edifice of variations.

The heart of this study is the relationship between the analysis of the finished work and its genesis in composition. Where the genesis and structure of the work intersect, each dependent on the other, is lodged the mysterious phenomenon of the creative process—the ultimate subject of investigation. In a sense, the point of this book is to show the nature of this interdependence, to inquire not only into what Beethoven did, but why he did it. The case is best made as part of a critical enterprise approaching the music through the concrete historical context embodied in the sketches as well as through analysis of the work itself. In some instances, in fact, there can be no clear separation between this historical context and its analytical relevance, inasmuch as significant implications of the sketches may be realized only in the finished composition. In this study, the full relevance of the genesis of the work is shown only in the analytical discussion in Part II, particularly in the

[7] Nottebohm, *Zweite Beethoveniana* (Leipzig, 1887; repr. New York, 1970), viii.

section on parody and in the final section of the analysis dealing with the last nine variations.

Important as well is the relationship between the Diabelli Variations and the other works of Beethoven's late style, particularly those written between 1819 and 1823. The most interesting of these is Beethoven's use or absorption—or self-parody—of the Arietta from the last Piano Sonata, Op. 111, in the Finale and coda of Op. 120. This relationship will be discussed in detail at the conclusion of the analytical section; it is the culmination of a complex musical evolution in which the Arietta, itself influenced by Beethoven's preoccupation with the Diabelli project, becomes a compositional model for the last of the Variations. Not only can we recognize the presence of material from the Arietta, but more than that, Beethoven executes in the Variations a kind of synopsis of elements from the entire Arietta hinging around a specific climactic passage. In the fourth variation of the Arietta, Beethoven achieved the effect of simultaneous harmonic and temporal suspension by ingenious manipulation of the musical parameters of pitch and rhythm. When he finished the Variations one year after completing the sonata, Beethoven incorporated a variant of this idea into his coda, establishing a relation between them more intimate than exists between any other of his larger works. This shows how possible it is to discover undetected ramifications even of a celebrated piece of music which has entered the main stream not only of Western music, but of general intellectual culture. And indeed, the Arietta deserves its reputation if we are to judge from Beethoven himself, who in his last extended work for piano drew upon the passage that, perhaps more than any other, captures the sense of the transcendent rendered imminent through the power of the human spirit.

PART I: THE PROCESS OF COMPOSITION

I. The Interrupted Genesis of the Variations

THE greatest of Beethoven's independent sets of variations owes its existence to an external stimulus: Anton Diabelli's project to collect variations of a theme of his own invention from the fifty finest *Tonsetzer* and *Virtuosen* of the Austrian empire. Diabelli's call must have been made in the early months of 1819, for the first dated contribution, that from Beethoven's former pupil Carl Czerny, bears the inscription '7. May, 1819'.[1] Beethoven's monumental set, on the other hand, was not completed until the spring of 1823. There is ample evidence, however, that its composition was under way fully four years before. While at Mödling during the summer of 1819, Beethoven was hard at work on the *Missa Solemnis*, Op. 123,[2] and his early sketches for the Mass in the Wittgenstein Sketchbook, today one of the treasures of the Beethoven-Archiv in Bonn, directly followed sketches for the Variations. This implies that Beethoven's early work on Op. 120 took place in the spring of 1819.

Beethoven's labours on the *Missa Solemnis* represent a *terminus ad quem* for his early work on the Diabelli Variations. Sketches for Op. 123 occupy not only most of the Wittgenstein Sketchbook, but also large portions of the next two desk-sized sketchbooks used by Beethoven during the years 1820-2, the Berlin manuscripts Artaria 195 and Artaria 197.[3] As these sketchbooks show, the composition of the Mass was interrupted by the Piano Sonata, Op. 109 and the Bagatelles, Op. 119 in 1820-1, and by the Piano Sonatas, Opp. 110 and 111 in 1821-2.

Only after the virtual completion of the Mass in mid-1822 do sketches again appear for the Diabelli Variations. No sketches for Op. 120 are to be found in any of the several pocket sketchbooks or numerous other pocket leaves devoted to the Mass.[4] It is only at the end of the Artaria 201 Sketchbook,

---

[1] See Georg Kinsky, *Das Werk Beethovens*, ed. H. Halm (Munich and Duisburg, 1955), p. 348.

[2] In early June of 1819 Beethoven writes to the Archduke Rudolph: 'The day on which a High Mass composed by me will be performed during the ceremonies solemnized for Your Imperial Highness will be the most glorious day of my life', and by August he writes again to Rudolph: 'But I hope to complete the Mass and in good time too, so that, if the arrangement still stands, it can be performed on the 19th.' Schindler testified that Beethoven worked intensely on the Mass during the summer of 1819, and in this case all the evidence seems to support him.

[3] The chronology of these sources has been analysed recently by Robert Winter in *The Beethoven Sketchbooks: History, Reconstruction, Inventory*, by Winter, Alan Tyson and Douglas Johnson (Berkeley and Oxford, 1985).

[4] Three pocket sketchbooks for Op. 123, housed in Bonn, have been published in facsimile

following late sketches for the Agnus of the Mass and the Overture, *Die Weihe des Hauses*, that work on Op. 120 finally resumes, and finds its completion in the Engelmann Sketchbook from 1823. In this sketchbook, indeed, as has been known since its publication in facsimile in 1913,[5] Beethoven actually also entered notes for proof corrections of the published opus. The detailed evidence from Beethoven's sketchbooks points towards a particularly intriguing aspect of the compositional history of the Diabelli Variations. We are dealing here with an exceptional case, in which Beethoven brought a major work to a relatively advanced stage in composition, and then laid it aside for a period of several years before returning to complete it.

The work Beethoven accomplished on the Variations in 1819 was far greater than is indicated by the Wittgenstein Sketchbook alone. Yet because of the fragmentary nature of the principal sketch sources—including the Wittgenstein Sketchbook itself—the extent of Beethoven's early work on Op. 120 passed unnoticed by generations of scholars. When Gustav Nottebohm surveyed the Op. 120 sketches a century ago, he observed that '[they] are housed in various locations and written for the most part on loose leaves, and what these contain only enables us to glimpse isolated moments in composition'.[6] It is evident from Nottebohm's essay that he knew neither the Wittgenstein Sketchbook nor the Engelmann Sketchbook, nor certain other loose sketchleaves of importance.[7] With only a small scattered selection of sketches available to him, Nottebohm was led into error about the chronology of two major sketch sources, Paris 77A and Landsberg 10, which he assumed were late in composition.

That other giant of nineteenth-century Beethoven scholarship, Alexander Wheelock Thayer, magnified the same error, and perpetrated a misconception that now has wide currency as fact.[8] Thayer believed that the main work on the Variations took place in the year 1822.[9] His argument relies heavily on Anton's Schindler's story that Beethoven's conception of the work grew from six or seven to twenty-five, and finally thirty-three variations.[10] However, if Schindler's story contains any truth whatsoever (as we shall see, it does

and transcription by Joseph Schmidt-Görg, as *Drei Skizzenbücher zur Missa Solemnis* (Bonn, 1952–70).

[5] *Receuil Thématique/de L. v. Beethoven./Autographe/contenant 37 pages de musique./Donné à Mr. Artôt (célèbre violoniste français)/par Mr. Auguste Artaria, éditeur des ouvrages de/Beethoven, à Vienne le 19 Mai 1835 (Leipzig, 1913).* (Wilhelm Engelmann Verlag: Leipzig, 1913).

[6] Nottebohm, *Zweite Beethoveniana* (Leipzig, 1887; repr. New York, 1970), p. 568.

[7] On the other hand, it is also clear from Nottebohm's essay that we still possess all of the sketch sources that he saw in the nineteenth century.

[8] Maynard Solomon writes in his biography of Beethoven that the composer produced most of Op. 120 in 1822 (*Beethoven* (New York, 1977), p. 265), and the same error is reproduced in many recent works about Beethoven.

[9] Thayer, *Life of Beethoven*, ed. Elliot Forbes (Princeton, 1964), p. 853.

[10] Schindler, *The Life of Beethoven* (repr. Mattapan, Mass., 1966), pp. 221–2.

parallel, perhaps coincidentally, features of Beethoven's sketches which Schindler may have noticed after the fact), it is totally incorrect as a guide to chronology. Beethoven's sketches and drafts from 1819 show clearly that the Diabelli Variations were planned on a very large scale even then, and as we shall see, it was not until the end of 1822 and the first months of 1823 that he returned to the Variations and finished them.

Only recently has it become possible to re-evaluate the older accepted chronology in light of the expanded knowledge of sources and more sophisticated techniques of the new sketch research. The outlines of the true chronology were first perceived by Robert Winter, and articulated in his review of the recent publication, in facsimile and transcription, of the Wittgenstein Sketchbook:[11] 'The mystery of the genesis of the Variations deepens with the revelation that fully nineteen of the thirty-three were apparently sketched before Beethoven abruptly set them aside to devote almost three years to the composition of the *Missa* and the last piano sonatas.'[12] For Paris 77A and Landsberg 10 consist of variation drafts comprising nineteen numbered variations. Actually, as we shall see, the large Draft of which Landsberg 10 forms a part includes even more variations, which deepens the mystery still further as to why Beethoven should have laid the work aside.

The divided chronology of the genesis of Op. 120 has far-reaching implications. We shall deal with the musical ramifications of this chronology later, but first we shall need to examine all the evidence in detail, in order to reconstruct, as much as is possible, each stage in the genesis of the Variations.

Two pieces of documentary evidence from 1820 corroborate the evidence of the sketches. In a letter to the publisher Simrock dated February 20th,[13] Beethoven offers 'Grosse Veränderungen über einen bekannten Deutschen', which can only refer to the Diabelli Variations. And in a conversation book from the beginning of April, Franz Oliva writes:[14]

Sie haben ja grössere Variationen angefangen, sind die nicht fertig geworden.

* * *

Diabelli würde viel geben.

That both of these references contain the implication of plurality, of 'Grosse Veränderungen', is significant. Like the 'Grosse Sonata', Op. 106, and the *Grosse Fuge*, the Variations overshadow, in their immensity, all Beethoven's previous efforts in this genre. And by the summer of 1819, about half a year after the completion of the great 'Hammerklavier' Sonata, plans and drafts for

[11] *L. van Beethoven: Ein Skizzenbuch zu den Diabelli-Variationen und zur Missa Solemnis*, SV 154, ed. J. Schmidt-Görg (Bonn, Facsimile, 1968, transcription, 1972).
[12] *Journal of the American Musicological Society*, xxviii (1975), p. 138.
[13] Emily Anderson, *The Letters of Beethoven* (New York, 1961),L. 1005.
[14] *Ludwig van Beethovens Konversationshefte*, 2, ed. Karl-Heinz Köhler and Dagmar Beck (Leipzig, 1976), p. 40.

fully two-thirds of the Diabelli Variations had already been written. Or more correctly, a large variation set had been fashioned in the rough which, years later, after having been expanded from within, became the work we know today.

Another letter of Beethoven's, from exactly the period in question, makes a reference, or at least a veiled allusion, to what are probably the Diabelli Variations. In early June 1819, in the first of his letters in which he refers to the *Missa Solemnis*, Beethoven writes to the Archduke Rudolph: 'Meanwhile in my writing-desk there are several compositions which bear witness to my remembering Y. I. H. [Your Imperial Highness]; and I hope to work them all out under more favourable conditions.'[15] Beethoven's sketches and drafts for Op. 120 should indeed have occupied the drawers of that writing-desk in June of 1819; and with those in mind his mention of 'remembering Y. I. H.' makes good sense. Rudolph was not only a contributor himself to Diabelli's collection, but he was the author of a large set of forty variations just then completed under Beethoven's tutelage.[16] If this letter in fact refers to Op. 120, then the Variations must have been put aside by early June, perhaps shortly after Beethoven's move to Mödling for his summer stay on 12 May. The available evidence admits no more detailed chronology.

Let us turn our attention now to an investigation into the contents of Beethoven's sketches for Op. 120.[17] A list of the sources to be treated, with their classification in the standard catalogue of sketches compiled by Hans Schmidt,[18] is shown in Table 1.

The Paris MSS 58B and 96, although listed by Schmidt, are not identified by him as containing sketches for Op. 120, and his breakdown of individual variations sketched in his other sources is not entirely complete or accurate. Furthermore, three additional sources are omitted from the catalogue: the single leaf Artaria 180/200 pp. 35–6, which has been identified by Winter, the Paris 57 manuscript, which has been identified by Brandenburg, and another single leaf containing Beethoven's copy of Diabelli's theme as well as sketches for several variations, which is now attached to the autograph of Op. 120.

---

[15] Anderson, L. 948.

[16] In the spring of 1818, Beethoven presented the Archduke with a theme, 'O Hoffnung', and the assignment of writing variations. Within the year the forty variations were completed, and through Beethoven's influence they were subsequently published, in the autumn of 1819, by Steiner as *Aufgabe/von Ludwig van Beethoven gedichtet/Vierzig Mahl verändert/und ihrem Verfasser gewidmet/von/seinem Schuler*. The genesis and publication of these variations thus overlap with Beethoven's 1819 work on Op. 120, and their chronological proximity suggests that Beethoven's interest in Diabelli's project could have had links with his pedagogical and personal connection with the Archduke.

[17] For the present study I have had access to transcriptions of most of the larger sketch sources for Op. 120, made by the late Prof. Erich Hertzmann. These were kindly lent to me by Prof. Daniel Heartz at the University of California at Berkeley.

[18] Schmidt, 'Verzeichnis der Skizzen Beethovens', *Beethoven-Jahrbuch*, vi, Jg. 1965/68 (1969), pp. 7–128.

TABLE 1. Sources of Beethoven's Diabelli Variations

Manuscript	Location	Date	Schmidt. No.
1. Leaf housed with Autograph	German private collection (formerly Koch–Flörsheim Collection)	1819	—
2. Paris 58B (= No. 2) fols. 1^r–2^v	Paris, Bibliothèque Nationale	1819	208
3. Paris 77A	Paris, Bibliothèque Nationale	1819	229
4. Paris 77B	Paris, Bibliothèque Nationale	1819	229
5. Witgenstein Sketchbook fols. 3^v–9^r, 10^v–11^r	Bonn, Beethoven-Archiv	1819	154
6. Landsberg 10 Sketch Miscellany pp. 165–76	West Berlin, Staatsbibliothek preussischer Kulturbesitz	1819	64
7. Montauban Fragment	Musée Ingres, Montauban, France	1819	341
8. Artaria 180/200 pp. 35–6	East Berlin, Deutsche Staatsbibliothek	1819	13
9. Artaria 201 Sketchbook pp. 123–5	West Berlin, Staatsbibliothek preussischer Kulturbesitz	1822	14
10. Paris 57, fols. 1^r, 2^r	Paris, Bibliothèque Nationale	1823	207
11. Paris 96, fols. 1^r–2^r	Paris, Bibliothèque Nationale	1823	248
12. Engelmann Sketchbook pp. 2–6; 16–18; 30–7	Bonn, Beethoven-Archiv	1823	107
13. Autograph	German private collection (formerly Koch–Flörsheim Collection)	1823	—

These sources have recently been incorporated into a more detailed inventory of sketches compiled by Brandenburg, and printed as an appendix to the monograph on the Variations by Arnold Münster.[19] In sum, including the autograph, there are thirteen extant sketch manuscripts for the Variations. Not surprisingly, many of these belong together as fragments of much larger manuscripts originally kept together by Beethoven. Once reconstructed,[20] this bewildering array of sources presents a remarkably coherent picture of Beethoven's compositional process.

[19] See Münster, *Studien zu Beethovens Diabelli-Variationen* (Munich, 1982), pp. 215–26. The sketches are briefly mentioned in this study but their implications for the structure of the finished work are not explored. See, for instance, pp. 184–8.

[20] The basic principles of source reconstruction of Beethoven's manuscripts are outlined by Douglas Johnson and Alan Tyson, 'Reconstructing Beethoven's Sketchbooks', *Journal of the American Musicological Society*, xxv (1972), pp. 137 ff. Tyson has since exemplified this procedure in separate articles on two sketchbooks. See his studies 'A Reconstruction of the Pastoral Symphony Sketchbook', *Beethoven Studies*, i, ed. Alan Tyson (New York, 1973, pp. 67–96; 'Das Leonore Skizzenbuch (Mendelssohn 15): Probleme der Rekonstruktion und Chronologie', *Beethoven Jahrbuch*, ix, Jg. 1973/77 (1977), pp. 469–500.

II. The Early Sketches (1819)

PARIS 58B (VARS. 3–7, 30)

IN his article, 'Beethovens "Erste Entwürfe" zu Variationenzyklen',[1] Sieghard Brandenburg has observed that for almost all Beethoven's variation works a series of hastily-written, spontaneous ideas for variations can be found among the sketches, often as a series of incipits which are subsequently worked out at length in the next layer of sketches. This description applies perfectly to what are evidently Beethoven's first sketches for Op. 120, a set of pencil jottings on a loose bifolium now known as the Paris manuscript 58B. These appear to be the earliest of the known sketches for Op. 120. For the first two incipits, when taken up into the large draft contained in the Paris 77A manuscript, to be discussed below, already have lost some of the close connection with Diabelli's theme which is evident in Paris 58B.[2]

These earliest ideas for a variation set on Diabelli's waltz are written on the present p. 4 (2^v) of the bifolium, and continue, after 'Var 6', onto the next facing page with a sketch for a 'minore' variation. The notation '2te V. in Mo[11]' implies that even at this stage Beethoven contemplated writing more than one slow variation in the minor, though all of the material actually sketched seems to relate to a single variation.[3] Transcribed by Nottebohm, portions of these sketches were published in *Zweite Beethoveniana*.[4] Nottebohm, however, neglected to designate the last sketch as a 'minore' variation, and even suppressed Beethoven's three-flat signature. These seven variation sketches are transcribed in full in Ex. 1. As Nottebohm pointed out, the first, second, and sixth of these sketches eventually evolved into Vars. 3, 4, and 7 of the finished work. Characteristically, Nottebohm cited only the most obvious derivations from these early sketches. Had he searched for more remote derivations, he might have added that more loosely the fourth, fifth,

---

[1] *Bericht über den Internationalen Musikwissenschaftlichen Kongress, Bonn 1970* (Kassel, 1971), pp. 335–57.

[2] It is by no means clear that all of the entries in Paris 58B were made before Beethoven had begun also to use other larger sketch sources, because some of the entries correspond very closely, even exactly, to sketches made in the Wittgenstein Sketchbook and other papers used contemporaneously with it.

[3] I am indebted to Sieghard Brandenburg for transcribing this inscription, which is very difficult to read.

[4] pp. 568–9.

Ex. 1

and last of the sketches anticipated Vars. 5, 6, and 30; only the third sketch, in which the opening measures are sharply divided in register, was left undeveloped as the set took more definite shape. In the fourth sketch, it is the marked iambic rhythm and ascending motive of a fourth that are retained (features shared by related early sketches for what became Var. 7). In the fifth, it is the far-ranging arpeggios, in the seventh, the imitative entries at the octave in the minor, the dotted rhythm, and the time signature. The development of all three of these ideas can be followed in Beethoven's subsequent sketches, that of the 'minore' with considerable clarity.

The third, unused sketch is interesting in another way. Although Beethoven abandoned the notion of setting the first measure of the theme in contrast with the following bars, he did exploit various kinds of contrast between the two parts of each variation half (the first eight bars to the next eight). The Op. 120 sketches show that this aspect of internal contrast within variations, notably in Var. 21, where these two halves are eventually given different time signatures, cost Beethoven considerable effort.

We have not yet considered the format and context of these first sketches for Op. 120. The Paris 58B bifolium consists of upright 16-stave paper, which was not used for any of the other surviving Variations sketches. In fact, only one other specimen of this paper type survives from this period,[5] and it was used latest by early 1819, since it contains material for the Ten National Airs Varied for Piano with Flute or Violin accompaniment, Op. 107, which were published in that year. In Paris 58B, early sketches for the Kyrie and Gloria of the Mass can also be found, several staves below the pencil sketches for the 'minore'. Beethoven seems to have been contemplating the Mass even as he made his first sketches for the Variations.

Another entry for Op. 120 on fol. 1[r], written in ink above the notations for the Mass, was probably made later, perhaps after Beethoven had begun to compose in the larger formats of the Wittgenstein Sketchbook and a set of loose papers that he kept together with his copy of Diabelli's theme. The same holds for sketches to several variations which fill the whole of fol. 1[v] of Paris 58B, on the other side of the spread-out bifolium as it was used by Beethoven. All of these sketches appear again in almost identical form in the Wittgenstein Sketchbook; indeed, certain notations among them are found in as many as four other places among Beethoven's early sketches for Op. 120. It is of course possible that all of these sketches were made first in Paris 58B, and subsequently copied into other sources. But the process may conceivably have gone the other way, especially because the list of incipits in Paris 58B provided a guide to orientation to which Beethoven may have referred in the process of working out his plan in detail. This brings us to the matter of the intimate interdependence of the sketch sources, and the origins of that interdependence in Beethoven's habits of sketching.

THE 1819 DRAFT (AUTOGRAPH, PARIS 77A, LANDSBERG 10, MONTAUBAN)

In his article, 'Plans for the Structure of the String Quartet in C sharp Minor, Op. 131',[6] Robert Winter has drawn attention to the fact that Beethoven, in composing the late quartets, not only used standard-format and pocket-format sketchbooks for use at home and afield, but also utilized loose bifolia and gathered sheets organized in four-stave systems. Winter calls these loose sketches, which were used contemporaneously with sketchbooks, 'score sketches', and traces their use for the late quartets to Beethoven's own professed deepening interest in part-writing problems.

Sketches or drafts in this format are by no means limited to the late quartets, and seem to represent an outgrowth of Beethoven's tendency, in

[5] This manuscript is a bifolium housed in the Vienna Gesellschaft der Musikfreunde as MS A49.

[6] *Beethoven Studies*, ii, ed. Alan Tyson (London, 1977), pp. 106–8. For a more comprehensive discussion of the genesis of the quartet see Winter's monograph *Compositional Origins of Beethoven's Opus 131* (Ann Arbor, 1982).

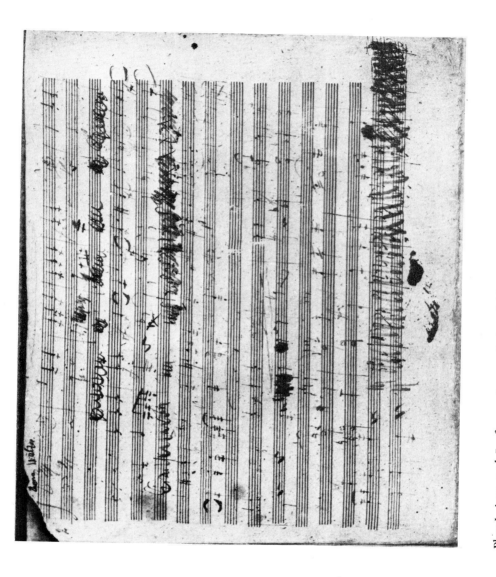

Plate I. Autograph Leaf, recto. A transcription of this manuscript is provided in Part III, Fig. I.

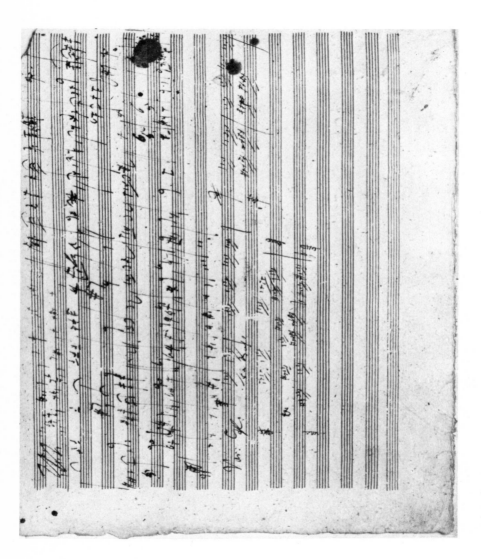

Plate II. Autograph Leaf, verso. A transcription of this sketchleaf is provided in Part III, Fig. 2.

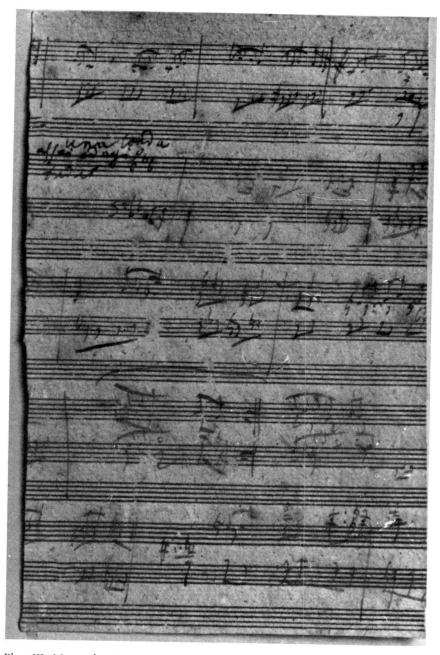

Plate III. Montauban Fragment, recto. A transcription of this sketchleaf is provided in Part III, Fɪɢ. 20.

Plate IV. Montauban Fragment, verso. A transcription of this sketchleaf is provided in Part III, Fig. 21.

earlier years, to make 'continuity drafts' for extended sections of works in progress.[7] While the earlier 'continuity drafts' were generally made in standard-format sketchbooks, the ageing Beethoven tended to segregate them on loose papers, while utilizing sketchbooks for the detailed working-out of material. Thus, some of these late 'continuity drafts' on loose bifolia and gathered sheets begin to approach the character of a preliminary autograph, however rough, and the sketchbooks used contemporaneously with them can show a surprisingly haphazard pattern of entries, since they provide only part of the record of Beethoven's compositional process. This practice can be no better illustrated than by Beethoven's early sketches and drafts for the Diabelli Variations.

As we have said, a large portion of Beethoven's early sketches for Op. 120 is contained in the Wittgenstein Sketchbook. Just as Winter observed about the late quartet sketchbooks, these sketches for Op. 120 can by no means be viewed in isolation. While Beethoven sketched in Wittgenstein, he worked as well on a set of drafts for the variations on loose papers, and close examination of both sources yields a wealth of internal evidence to prove that they are contemporaneous and interrelated documents. In fact, many sketches in Wittgenstein that are cryptic in themselves become intelligible in light of the loose drafts that accompany that sketchbook.[8]

This set of drafts comprises twenty-three variations in order, in addition to the copy of Diabelli's theme in Beethoven's hand. However, this source is no longer physically intact, and must be restored, at least in concept, from documents now housed in four different European collections. In view of its thorough dismemberment, it is indeed fortunate that enough has survived to permit its reconstruction at all.[9] Because of the complications attending this source; we shall need to treat it in considerable detail, in order to show each step in its reconstruction.

The first page of this source is none other than Beethoven's copy of Diabelli's theme, on a single leaf of 16-stave paper now preserved with the autograph of the Variations (see Plate I and the transcription in Part III, Fig. 1). The paper type of this leaf is identical to that used in the Wittgenstein Sketchbook, and bears the watermark 'C & I HONIG'.[10] This leaf contains

[7] The term 'continuity draft' stems from Joshua Rifkin, and was introduced to the literature by Lewis Lockwood in his article 'On Beethoven's Sketches and Autographs: Some Problems of Definition and Interpretation', *Acta musicologica*, xiii (1970), pp. 32–47.

[8] One reason for the inadequacy of the transcription published with the Beethoven-Haus edition is doubtless that the sketchbook was not treated in light of its related sketch sources in Paris, Berlin, and elsewhere.

[9] This may be an indication of the fate of other of Beethoven's drafts on loose papers which could have been more easily lost or dismembered, even in Beethoven's own time. One reason for the preponderance of these drafts for the late quartets may be that since they were composed in the years directly before Beethoven's death, they were less likely to have been misplaced or dispersed.

[10] This information was kindly supplied by Sieghard Brandenburg, who examined the

sketches from both of Beethoven's periods of composition on Op. 120 (1819 and 1822–3) but its identification with the basic 1819 Draft is shown by the fact that the rastrology of the verso of this leaf matches exactly with the rastrology of the first side, fol. 1ʳ, of the manuscript Paris 77A.[11]

The latter manuscript, a single bifolium, contains drafts, one to a side, for Vars. 3, 4, 9, and 10 of the final version.[12] Since sketch material for the intervening variations exists in Paris 58B and Wittgenstein, it is practically certain that a bifolium is missing from Paris 77A which originally formed a gathered sheet with it. Such a bifolium would be exactly the size necessary to hold Vars. 5, 6, 7, and 8, with one variation to a page.

Var. 10, since it is the first 'double' variation with both halves written out and which therefore cannot be contained on one side, continues from the last side of Paris 77A onto the first of Landsberg 10 (p. 165), a section of an autograph miscellany in West Berlin. The relevant portion of Landsberg 10 consists of a single bifolium and a whole gathered sheet, containing Vars. 10–14, 16–21, 22 (labelled 'Don Giovanni'), and an unused variation.

Finally, a sketchleaf fragment now housed at the Musée Ingres in Montauban, France, preserves what must be part of the second leaf of the bifolium or gathered sheet which followed the end of Landsberg 10. This leaf contains material for Vars. 27, 30, and 32, the Fugue in E flat. In the Wittgenstein Sketchbook, where material for most of these variation drafts can be found, sketches for the finale after the E flat Fugue are lacking, although one sketch, as we shall see, may suggest a plan for a finale to follow directly the slow minor variation, No. 30. It is uncertain, then, whether Beethoven's 1819 draft broke off after the Fugue, or contained a projected finale to the cycle.

In addition to the aforementioned manuscripts, an aborted continuation to a passage in Var. 21 in Landsberg 10 is preserved on a single leaf of the same paper type, now housed in East Berlin as the manuscript Artaria 180/200, pp. 35–6. This leaf contains only two bars for Var. 21, and then breaks off. The remainder of the leaf contains three bars of sketches relating loosely to Var. 15, and sketches for the Credo of the Missa Solemnis.

The greatest portion of Beethoven's draft, therefore, can be assembled from the first four manuscripts cited above, each of which is now attached to a different collection. These are shown in Table 2.

In the case of the autograph leaf, Paris 77A, and Landsberg 10, the correctness of this reconstruction is assured by identity of paper type and watermarks, and sketch continuity. The watermark common to these manuscripts contains the inscription 'C & I HONIG' beneath a coat of arms of a lily on a shield in quadrants 1 and 2, and the letters 'G K' in the right-hand corner in

manuscript in 1983. For the present study I have utilized photographs of the autograph supplied me by the Beethoven-Archiv in Bonn.

[11] This was determined by comparison of photographs at the Beethoven-Archiv in Bonn.

[12] Unless otherwise specified, all numbering of variations is according to the finished work.

TABLE 2. The Paris–Landsberg–Montauban Draft of 1819

Source		Material/Variation number
Op. 120 Autograph, fol. 1		Theme
Paris, BN, MS 77 pp. 1–4	1/2	{ var. 3 (1)* { var. 4 (2)
		var. 5 (3) lost bifolium var. 6 (4) vars. sketched var. 7 (5) in Wittgenstein var. 8 (6) sketchbook
	3/4	{ var. 9 (7) { var. 10 (8) beginning
Berlin, SPK, Landsberg 10 pp. 165–76**	165/66	{ var. 10 (8) cont. { var. 11 (9) { var. 12 (10)
	167/68	{ var. 12 (10) cont. { var. 13 (11) { var. 14 (12) beginning
	169/70	{ var. 14 (12) cont. { var. 16 (13) { var. 17 (14) beginning
	171/72	{ var. 17 (14) cont. { var. 18 (15) { var. 19 (16)
	173/74	{ var. 19 (16) cont. { var. 20 (17) { var. 21 (18) beginning
	175/76	{ var. 21 (18) cont. { var. 22 (not numbered by Beethoven) { var. X (unused; 19)
Montauban leaf fragment SV 341		var. 27 (20)
		var. 30 (21) ['minore']
		var. 32 (22) [fugue]

* The variations are given their final numbering, with the original number in parentheses.

** For the precise distribution of the variations in Landsberg 10, see Hans-Günter Klein, *Ludwig van Beethoven: Autographe und Abschriften*, Staatsbibliothek preussischer Kulturbesitz, Kataloge der Musikabteilung, 1/2 (Berlin, 1975), pp. 144–5.

quadrant 4. The Montauban leaf, however, has been cut in such a way that its watermark is not visible; therefore final justification for its association with Landsberg 10 must be sought on other grounds. This relation is shown not only by the sketch content but also by a system of numbering in pencil in Beethoven's hand that extends throughout the set of drafts and must have been made when they were still intact. The number '21' entered in pencil before the draft of the 'minore' variation (ultimately Var. 30) follows from the '9–19' found in Landsberg 10.[13] Further evidence is supplied by the provenance of the sketchleaf itself. According to the inscription on the panel where the leaf is mounted, it was given to the composer L. D. Besozzi by Prof. Franz Hauser (misspelt 'Hauzer' on the manuscript) at Vienna in 1840 (see Plate III and the transcription in Part III, Fig. 20). Besozzi subsequently offered it to the important French painter and amateur musician Jean-Auguste-Dominique Ingres; today it hangs in the gallery of the Ingres Museum in southern France at Montauban, the place of birth of the painter. Hauser was a famous singer and teacher at residence in Vienna from 1837; he was also an avid collector of music manuscripts. It seems likely that Hauser received the Montauban leaf from Ludwig Landsberg, who is known to have occasionally given away autographs. Finally, the sketch content of the Wittgenstein Sketchbook would lead us to postulate that the Montauban leaf was a part of the set of drafts even in the absence of other evidence, because the variations represented in Montauban are practically the only remaining variations from Wittgenstein that had not occurred in the Draft.

The importance of the Montauban fragment is considerable. It shows that Beethoven's Draft extended to the 'minore' variation and E flat Fugue—in other words, to the penultimate variations of the projected work. Beethoven's early plan for Op. 120, therefore, encompassed a complete cycle, with the exception of some sort of finale needed to follow the Fugue. Surviving sketches from the late period of composition for Op. 120 show that when Beethoven finally returned to the work, he concentrated his efforts on the Fugue and the transition to the Finale. This evidence matches well with the absence of finale sketches in Wittgenstein, and suggests that the Montauban fragment preserves parts of all the most essential features from the end of this set of early drafts.

Another problem of source reconstruction is presented by the Wittgenstein Sketchbook. As Robert Winter has pointed out in his review of the Beethoven-Haus edition of Wittgenstein, many leaves have been removed from it, including a whole series of leaves toward the back.[14] Two bifolia containing sketches for Op. 120 were also displaced, and these, now known as

---

[13] There is no break in the numbering system, since '21' is affixed to the 'minore' variation, while three bars of the preceding variation, which must have been '20', are preserved in Montauban.

[14] Winter, *Journal of the American Musicological Society*, xxviii (1975), pp. 135–8.

the Paris 77B MS, fit perfectly into the sketch sequence on the basis of paper type and musical content. Unfortunately, the Beethoven–Haus edition of this sketchbook failed to include MS 77B, and thus reproduces an obvious gap in the sketch progression from the present p. 10 to p. 11, where the Paris leaves belong.

Because of the many missing leaves in Wittgenstein, and the fact that the paper type used in this sketchbook is identical with that used in the Draft, it is tempting to suppose that the Draft may have once formed part of the Wittgenstein Sketchbook itself. This is impossible, however, because Wittgenstein is one of those Beethoven sketchbooks that consists of a single large gathering of leaves. The Paris–Landsberg–Montauban Draft, on the other hand, consists of a series of loose bifolia and gathered sheets (see Table 2 above), a format incompatible with the sketchbook. What the identify of paper type between these sources suggests is that when Beethoven acquired the Wittgenstein Sketchbook, he also obtained loose sheets of music-paper of the same type. This seems natural enough, considering his working methods. The identity of paper type is not sufficient by itself to fix the chronology of the musical contents of the Draft, on the other hand; but the correspondence in sketch content between Wittgenstein and Paris–Landsberg–Montauban is so intimate that it establishes this chronology beyond any reasonable doubt.

Early work for the Diabelli Variations is summarized in Fig. 1. As this shows, work on the Variations in the Wittgenstein Sketchbook is preceded and followed by entries for the Op. 107 Variations and for the *Missa Solemnis*, respectively. Apart from the earliest sketches in Paris 58B, all of Beethoven's early manuscripts for the Variations belong to the two reconstructed formats of the PLM Draft and the Wittgenstein Sketchbook.

The First Variation Drafts (Vars. 3, 4)

In retracing Beethoven's process of composition for Op. 120, we shall find that, in general, the sketchbook was used for the notation of new ideas and for the working-out of ideas already conceived, while the Paris-Landsberg-Montauban (PLM) Draft preserves a relatively clean copy for variations elaborated at full length. In some cases, Beethoven seems to have worked out a draft for a variation in the sketchbook, and subsequently copied it into its appointed place among the set of loose drafts. Beethoven arrived at this procedure only in the process of working, however, and began his labours without recourse to the sketchbook at all. In fact, Beethoven's earliest sketches, apart from the incipits in Paris 58B, appear to be those contained in Paris 77A for what were, at this stage, the first two variations.

This is not immediately obvious from the present appearance of these leaves, for what first meets the eye is the full-bodied texture of the drafts, which stands out against faint, sometimes scarcely-legible notations that have

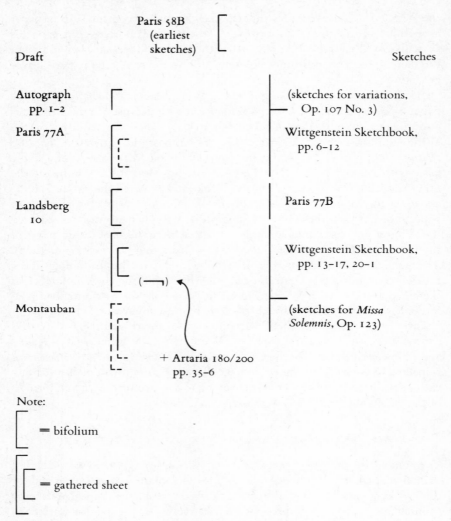

Dotted lines represent missing portions of the manuscripts.

FIG. 1. Summary of the early sketches

been written over and obscured in the process of composition. Close inspection reveals that there are three levels of composition recorded in these pages, in ink, pencil, and again in ink; that they all involve changes, elaboration, and refinements; and that all are in Beethoven's hand. The beginning of the earliest of these levels for the first variation of the draft (Var. 3, finished version), consisting of a sketch in two voices, is shown in Ex. 2, where it is juxtaposed with the primitive version in Paris 58B.

Ex. 2   Paris 58B

Paris 77A

This sketch already marks an advance. The four bars of unchanging tonic harmony at the beginning of the Paris 58B sketch yield to an alternation between tonic and dominant harmonies, and the movement of the bass in syncopation places emphasis on the normally weak second beat in the first three bars. This syncopation is more subtly carried into the melody by means of repeated tones at the beginning of bars, a device that Beethoven retained in the final version. Also significant is the change in the linear contour of the melody. The pencil sketch in Paris 58B already contains the idea of a descent from the upper third, E, but there the descent reaches its goal, G, prematurely, thus requiring an awkward repetition of the falling second A–G. A restructuring of this linear descent was begun when Beethoven worked in Paris 77A, for at the beginning of the second full bar the note C is crossed out and changed to D, a pattern that postpones the descent of the line, and produces a smoother melodic curve. The final stage in this process, the alteration of the A–G in bar 4 to G–F—which eliminates the repetition of this descending second to the dominant note—was not achieved until 1823, but it consists of but another refinement in the direction of the changes evident in Paris 77A. Moreover, Beethoven's setting for the beginning of the second half in the first layer of Paris 77A resembles his final solution still more closely, as Ex. 3 shows. Here the line is taken up still higher to F, but then descends in three consistent repetitions of the pattern of repeated notes, the last written as a tied A resolving to G. These problems of linear progression, of achieving a satisfactory melodic transformation of the musical fundaments supplied by Diabelli's theme, were basic issues confronting Beethoven in the sketches for the third variation.

Ex. 3

Even the opening turn, copied from Diabelli's theme, is transformed in these sketches for the third variation into something bearing some relationship with the substance of the variation. In Paris 77A it becomes a third straddling the tonic note, anticipating the third, C–E, with which the theme continues. In the final version of this variation Beethoven intensifies this idea by using the first four notes, spanning E–G, to anticipate the melodic descent contained in the first four bars (Ex. 4). The final solution, which is clearly superior to that in Paris 77A, is nevertheless consistent with it. The opening third at the beginning of Paris 77A is a signpost on the way toward the possibility discovered and achieved by Beethoven in the finished work.

Ex. 4

These observations about a single sketch already shed light on interesting facets of Beethoven's compositional process. First of all, Beethoven regards the theme critically as a reservoir of unrealized possibilities. The opening turn of Diabelli's theme, for example, has no connection with the material that follows it; it is merely a flourish for its own sake. It is therefore abandoned in Var. 3 and in many others, but when Beethoven does shift his attention to it he does so with a vengeance, as in Vars. 9 and 11, both of which are based *throughout* on the turn. If the turn could be exploited compositionally, and not left to stand as an unrealized possibility, it was quite suitable material for treatment.

Another example is the harmonic-rhythmic structure of the theme in its first four bars. Virtually nothing happens. The harmonic immobility of this passage is made obvious by ten repeated C major triads in the right hand; the bass, with its ascending fourths to C on strong beats is entirely lacking in subtlety of invention. Yet, as if in a last effort to render this material more interesting, Diabelli designated a crescendo to forte over these first four bars. It is revealing that Beethoven discards this crescendo at once and does not return to it. Essentially, as with the turn, it is in the theme without reason; it is unjustified by the nature of the material. In several cases, Beethoven does designate crescendos over each half of a variation, but in every case this intensification is reflected by the increasing activity of contrapuntal voices, or harmonic tension, or other means. Beethoven's treatment of his given theme and of his own preliminary sketches proceeds from a kind of principle of sufficient reason, in the form of energy that vitalizes and makes coherent material which lacks interest or purpose.

The next variation sketched in Paris 77A—Var. 4—shows the same tripartite working method as its predecessor; that is, Beethoven entered a draft in ink, added corrections once in pencil, and then again in ink. In both cases this practice of superimposing changes gradually produced a littered and partially-illegible manuscript, and this may have been one reason why Beethoven eventually turned to the Wittgenstein Sketchbook as the place to work out his ideas. It seems likely, however, that before putting any notations into Wittgenstein Beethoven might have drafted as far as Var. 6, since material for Vars. 5 and 6 is only fleetingly apparent in the sketchbook, which begins with an attempted draft for Var. 7.

We know from Paris 58B that even at the time of their original inception, several of the opening variations (or rather their prototypes) stood in the same order as they appear in the completed work. In the Diabelli Variations sketches, unlike the sketches for Op. 35,[15] for example, there was comparatively little reordering of the variations in the process of composition, apart from a few provisional numbers attached to variations sketched in Wittgenstein.[16] By the time Beethoven was ready to write out a rough draft for the Variations, he had already settled on the order in which they stand in the finished work.[17] It seems most probable that this was true also for Vars. 5 to 8 in the draft, but since they have been lost, this cannot be known with certainty. In any case, for only Vars. 5 and 6 do we have a real paucity of sketch material, presumably because Beethoven worked on these variations by superimposing changes on the draft itself, as in the two variations at the head of Paris 77A.

The draft for the prototype of Var. 5 in Paris 58B implies that the underlying idea for this variation was rhythmic, as in Var. 4. An iambic rhythm, emphasized by octave leaps, defines and unifies every bar in the variation half which Beethoven sketched all the way through. And although this variation underwent a profound evolution that is poorly documented by the surviving sketches, its rhythmic pulse remained unchanged from its earliest sketch in Paris 58B to the finished version. Still more interesting is the fact that the material used in the second half of this variation also found its way into Var. 7. This can be seen already in Paris 58B (see Ex. 1 above) and followed further in Wittgenstein. It is the first instance of a pervasive phenomenon in the Op. 120 sketches: the evolution of different variations, and sometimes drastically contrasting variations, from common material and ideas.

[15] See Christopher Reynolds, 'Beethoven's Sketches for the Variations in E^b Op. 35', *Beethoven Studies*, iii, ed. Alan Tyson (Cambridge, 1982), pp. 47–84.
[16] These are discussed below, pp. 39–40.
[17] Allowing, of course, for the internal expansion of the work through the addition of new variations in 1823.

THE EARLY WITTGENSTEIN SKETCHES (VARS. 7, 12, 18, 19, 21)

This process can be no better illustrated than by the very first entries for the Variations in the Wittgenstein Sketchbook. Beethoven begins his work in the sketchbook with an attempt at a draft for Var. 7. Just as in the Paris 77A drafts for Vars. 3 and 4, this sketch utilizes two staves and is worked out at the full length of thirty-two bars. In contrast to the previous drafts, however, Beethoven introduces new material in no way connected with his first inspiration in Paris 58B (cf. Ex. 1 above), in the form of a different continuation for the last eight bars of the first half (see Ex. 5). It is noteworthy that this new continuation, which was in the end rejected in favour of the older idea, itself became part of another variation, No. 12. Moreover, the idea for the above draft—that of a strong contrast between the robust octaves spanning five octaves in the first part, and the quieter figuration and dropping chromatic semitones of the second—eventually found realization in Var. 21. Relationships between variations in the finished work come into relief in these sketches, and these point towards affinities between variations that might easily be overlooked by a critic surveying the finished work alone.

Ex. 5

On the facing page, Wittgenstein fol. 4ʳ, Beethoven wrote two alternative continuations for the second part of the drafted variation, material that was eventually taken up in the second part of Var. 12. A comparison of this first continuation with its counterpart in the Landsberg 10 draft of Var. 12 reveals that only a slight modification was necessary to adapt this material to its new context (see Ex. 6). In Landsberg 10 Beethoven replaced the tied suspensions of the earlier sketch with the turn figure from Diabelli's theme, which is a pervasive feature of the entire variation.

Ex. 6   Wittgenstein Sketchbook

Landsberg 10

Another, more subtle relationship is perceptible between these drafts in Wittgenstein for what became part of Var. 12 and the creation of another variation, No. 18. The affinity between the finished Vars. 12 and 18 is evident in their common use of the turn figure expanded to a double turn. And in the sketchbook, we can trace a bond between these evolving variations through their relation to still another member of the set, Var. 19. (Because of the complexity of this relationship, the reader is advised to refer to the full transcription in Part III, Figs. 22-5.)

The end of the second alternative continuation on fol. 4^r resembles the final cadence for what became Var. 18 in its linear, sequential ascent to C in the highest register, and this similarity is particularly interesting in light of another sketch directly below in Wittgenstein, in the same texture of ink. This is a sketch for a variation in close imitation, a prototype for Var. 19 from the finished piece. In the reworking of Var. 19, a few pages later in Wittgenstein, these close imitative entries are expanded into a canon extending over the first eight bars, and the starting pitch for what now becomes a chain of arpeggios is raised an octave, to high C, a sonority which connects more organically with the lofty register of the preceding cadence (see Ex. 7). It appears that the coupling of Vars. 18 and 19 originated in a first impression of the composer and may well have been in part coincidental, just as any free association of ideas is, in a fundamental sense, accidental. What is not coincidental is Beethoven's development of the idea of close imitation on a short rhythmic figure into a wave of rhythmically extended points of canonic imitation spanning the compass of the keyboard, or his sensitivity to the transition in sonority between two interrelated but contrasting variations.

Ex. 7

All the sketches in these first two pages of Wittgenstein that have been discussed so far appear from the shade and texture of ink to have been made at about the same time. At some later point, after Beethoven had already filled several more pages in Wittgenstein with sketches for Op. 120, he returned to these first pages to revise and add material. These changes and additions, made in darker ink, continue the compositional process we have outlined above. Beethoven's next act was to reject the new continuation he had written to Var. 7 and to restore the Paris 58B sketch. This was copied into Wittgenstein, fol. 4ʳ, and hooked in by 'Vi = 100, – de 100' signs. With this reversion to the older material, the alternative continuation was broken free, to become the basis for Var. 12.

Beethoven then entered a new draft on the empty staves left at the bottom of fol. 3ᵛ which he was forced to continue on the lower staves of fol. 5ʳ, because all the other space on these pages had already been filled. This draft utilizes the rhythmic unit ♩♩ ♩♩ ♩ from the sketch prototype for Var. 19, and the chromatic auxiliary notes from the sketch for Var. 12, and combines these in a highly original fashion to create a draft for Var. 18. This variation seems to have been conceived specifically as the predecessor to the fast canonic variation, No. 19, for Beethoven wrote at the end of the draft on fol. 5ʳ, 'Vi — Var 2', while the notation 'Var: 2' is attached to the variation prototype for No. 19. This shows that Var. 18 was composed intentionally as a companion for Var. 19; for Beethoven, these two variations, like Nos. 3 and 4, seem to have been associated together and planned in sequence.

It is hazardous, however, to attribute too much weight to this coupling of adjacent variations. For example, a notation at the bottom of Landsberg 10, p. 170, shows that Beethoven contemplated placing either the present Var. 18 *or* the present Var. 27 after the march-pair of variations, Nos. 16–17. At this point, both 18 and 27 were 'presto' variations, and evidently were to some degree interchangeable.

The most significant point uncovered by our study of the Wittgenstein Sketchbook thus far concerns the closely connected genesis of groups of variations for the most part widely separated in the variation order. The first variation drafted in the sketchbook, as we have seen, contains the seeds for the finished Vars. 7, 12, and 21, and represents, in a sense, the ancestor of all three. Similarly, in the Paris 58B prototype of Var. 4, we can see the idea subsequently used in Var. 7, while Var. 18 evidently arose from Beethoven's meditation on ideas akin to those in his drafts for 12 and 19. A subtle matrix of relationships is held in common by these variations, and provides evidence of the cogency of Beethoven's insight into the potential of basic musical elements.

THE RELATION OF SKETCHES AND DRAFT

Let us pause at this point in our analysis of the sketches in order to assess the relationship between the entries in Wittgenstein and the corresponding drafts in PLM. The draft for Var. 18 in the sketchbook, which was entered after at least several pages of sketches had been made in Wittgenstein, provides evidence that the set of loose drafts were not always used simultaneously with the sketchbook. For on p. 168 of Landsberg 10, beneath the draft for Var. 14,

Beethoven writes: 'maestoso als dann ♪♪♪ ' which

implies that much work on Var. 18 had been executed in Wittgenstein before this same material was channelled into its place in the draft of the whole. Many of these variations also show corrections and improvements when taken up into the draft; this is true of the eleventh, the sixteenth, and the eighteenth variations among others; and in the eighteenth this is particularly obvious since two bars that were copied from Wittgenstein are crossed out and re-written. In the case of Var. 19, which reaches a relatively polished form even in Wittgenstein, the draft entry is actually abbreviated, in that only one voice of the two-voiced canon is written out, the other omitted but understood. On the other hand, Beethoven's changes in the draft are never so great as to imply a chronological gap between these sources or even to imply that much actual composition took place in Landsberg 10 and Montauban. The bulk of Beethoven's creative labour took place in Wittgenstein, and its record is frequently laconic, poorly legible, and difficult to interpret. The easily-legible drafts represent work for the most part one step removed from creation itself, made after a store of ideas had been accumulated.

The chronological sequence in composition is shown in Fig. 2. After pre-liminary sketching, Beethoven started sustained work with the loose drafts, soon abandoned them for the sketchbook, and finished the Draft only after he had, in most cases, executed preliminary work in the sketchbook.

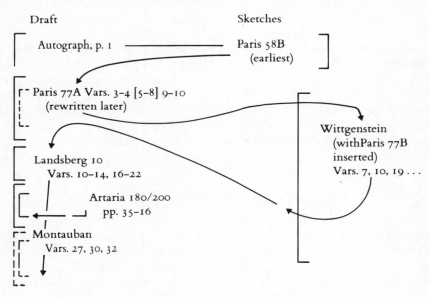

FIG. 2. The chronological sequence in composition

We can broadly distinguish three stages in composition here, stages that Beethoven himself seems to have kept separate. The first stage consists of the spontaneous impressions and ideas hastily notated in Paris 58B, the second the laborious working-out and derivation of material in the first two levels of Paris 77A and Wittgenstein, the third the organization of a macroscopic set of drafts embracing the whole work in PLM. Robert Winter's assessment of Beethoven's use of different sketch formats for the late quartets, that 'the days on which Beethoven worked on only one of these formats and not on the others were rare indeed'[18] does not seem to apply too well to the Op. 120 sketches, for Beethoven seems to have gone far towards completing one stage of composition, as expressed in one 'format', before proceeding to the next. Wittgenstein and the PLM Draft, sources that correspond intimately and cast much light upon one another, were nevertheless, it would seem, written successively.

There are two variations in these drafts for which virtually no material appears in Wittgenstein: the first 'minore', No. 9, and the slow 'maestoso' variation with double-dotted rhythms, No. 14. Both of these drafts are conspicuously rough; doubtless Beethoven returned to the practice with which he began these drafts, that of composing immediately in them without preliminary sketching in Wittgenstein. This might have occurred after most of the notations were made in the sketchbook, when Beethoven set out to organize his thoughts as an intelligible, continuous draft.

It is also of course possible that sketches are missing for these variations, sketches that could have existed at the beginning of the present sketchbook, for example, or elsewhere. It may be relevant in this connection that few sketches are to be found in Wittgenstein for certain other variations, such as Nos. 10 and 13. But though this possibility cannot be totally discounted, there is also too little evidence of missing sketches to justify the assumption of a lost source. There are no conspicuous gaps in the drafts apart from the bifolium from Paris 77A and the remainder of Montauban, and none at all in Wittgenstein, once the Paris leaves are added; and if such a gap did exist, it would disrupt the close correspondence between the two principal sketch formats. This correspondence and the transference of material from sketchbook to drafts is shown in Fig. 3. As this shows, this correspondence tightens toward the end of the Draft. The last eleven entries in Landsberg and Montauban are sketched in Wittgenstein, and nearly all of the material in the sketchbook is utilized. The close affinity in content between Wittgenstein and PLM, in conjunction with the identity of their paper types, provides persuasive evidence that the Draft was made by the summer of 1819, as part of the burst of activity that also produced Paris 58B and the sketches in Wittgenstein.[19]

---

[18] Winter, 'Plans for the Structure of the String Quartet in C sharp Minor, Op. 131', p. 108.

[19] Nottebohm's mistake in attributing Landsberg 10 to 1822 resulted from the fact that he saw neither the Wittgenstein Sketchbook nor the Montauban fragment, nor the autograph of Op. 120. Since the first sketches made by Beethoven after the long interruption in composition are not more advanced than Landsberg 10, Nottebohm assumed that these drafts must be contemporary with the Sketchbook Artaria 201.

Sketchbook   PLM Draft/Variation number

                                                     3

                                                     4
related ideas, no draft ─ ─ ─ ─ ─ ─ ─ ─ ─► [5]
                                                              missing
related ideas, no draft ─ ─ ─ ─ ─ ─ ─ ─ ─► [6]

sketches and full draft ───────────────► [7]
                                                              bifolium
sketches and full draft ───────────────► [8]

(no material)   9

incipit only ─ ─ ─ ─ ─ ─ ─ ─ ─ ─ ─ ─ ─► 10

two attempts at draft ──────────────► 11

ideas mixed with draft for VII ──────► 12

a few bars only ─ ─ ─ ─ ─ ─ ─ ─ ─ ─ ─► 13

(no material)   14

ideas for both parts   (15 not in PLM)

full draft ──────────────────────► 16 (abbreviated)

incipit only ──────────────────────► 17

sketches and full draft ───────────► 18

two full drafts ───────────────────► 19 (abbreviated)

related ideas ─ ─ ─ ─ ─ ─ ─ ─ ─ ─ ─► 20

first part ──────────────────────► 21

principal idea ──────────────────► 22

a few bars only ─────────────────► unused Var.

first half   (26 not in PLM)

related ideas ─ ─ ─ ─ ─ ─ ─ ─ ─ ─ ─► 27

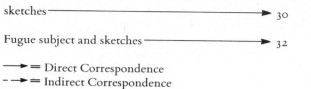

sketches ──────────────────────▶ 30

Fugue subject and sketches ──────────▶ 32

──▶ = Direct Correspondence
- ─▶ = Indirect Correspondence

FIG. 3. The correspondence between sketches and draft

ASPECTS OF BEETHOVEN'S COMPOSITIONAL PROCESS (VARS. 1, 15, 16, 19–22, 28)

The following discussion is an attempt to analyse further some of the most striking musical implications of the reconstructed Wittgenstein Sketchbook and the PLM Draft. Detailed description of this material would be superfluous—an annotated transcription of both sources is supplied in Part III, Figs 1–39. Nor can the analysis of sketches always take the form of a systematic argument following a pre-ordained methodology. These sketches demand interpretation, but on their own terms. The central concern here, as elsewhere, is with Beethoven's creative process, as reflected by the problems, vicissitudes, and internal stages of composition.

In general, it is striking how little of the material in Wittgenstein goes unused in the loose drafts and, ultimately, in the finished piece. Most of the sketches, if they do not obviously relate to one of the finished variations, are related clearly enough to the development of ideas used in one, or, most often, several of the finished variations. Still, there are a few entries in Wittgenstein that were subsequently abandoned. The most interesting of these is found on one of the final pages of work on Op. 120 contained in the sketchbook, where Beethoven considers plans for an improvisatory introduction to the theme (see Ex. 8). It seems that the work was going to begin with a fantasy on the motivic fourth from the outset of Diabelli's theme. The introduction then terminated with a cadenza over a supertonic pedal resolving, after a flurry of dominant trills, to the theme. Beethoven had used such an introductory preface to a set of variations in his Choral Fantasia of 1808, and subsequently in his Variations on the Song 'Ich bin der Schneider Kakadu' for Piano Trio, Op. 121a, whereas similar elaborations for solo piano are found at the beginnings of the Concerto in E flat, Op. 73, and the unfinished Piano Concerto of 1815.[20] Another example of such an introduction, from exactly the time in question, is provided by the Archduke Rudolph's 40 Variations on the Theme 'O Hoffnung', composed under Beethoven's supervision (see p. 6 above, n. 16). It is interesting that Beethoven considered that possibility for Op. 120, only to discard it. Perhaps he concluded that Diabelli's theme was too slight to

[20] See Lewis Lockwood, 'Beethoven's Unfinished Piano Concerto of 1815: Sources and Problems', *Musical Quarterly*, lvi (1970), pp. 624–46.

Ex. 8

follow the arresting, rhetorical gestures implicit in such an introduction. In any event, Beethoven rejected the idea of an introduction, but he did eventually place a striking gesture near the beginning of the set in the form of the opening march variation.

This first variation of the thirty-three was evidently not composed until 1823. But one of the few sketches in Wittgenstein left unused in the drafts (Ex. 9) surely represents a prototype for Var. 1.

Ex. 9

This sketch is a march of majestic character, reminding us, for example, of the introduction to the Overture, *Die Weihe des Hauses* composed in 1822. It is fascinating that Beethoven should have developed the idea of a march suggestive of a French overture once he had rejected plans for the introduction. (One is reminded of Bach's use of the French overture at the beginning of the second half of the Goldberg Variations.) There is something problematical about opening a monumental set of variations with a trivial waltz. Instead of the gentle Var. 3, sketched in Paris 58B, etc., Beethoven ultimately started with a vigorous march, Alla marcia maestoso. This greatly strengthens the beginning of the work, lending to it the effect of grand anticipation. We shall have occasion later to examine this matter in considerable detail, in connection with the overall formal progression of the Diabelli Variations (see below pp. 172–5).

Material for another variation omitted from Landsberg 10 but included in the final version—No. 15—can also be found in Wittgenstein. A distinctive aspect of this variation is the chromatic progression in the second half of the first part, which brings a return to the tonic. This can already be found on fol. 6ᵛ of the sketchbook (see Ex. 10). The only differences between this sketch and the finished version lie in the metre (3/4 instead of 2/4) and the cadence, which turns at the last moment to the dominant, rather amusingly (or was it absent-mindedly?). In the final version of this variation, which is only attained in the Engelmann Sketchbook from the spring of 1823, Beethoven treats the augmented-sixth chord four bars from the cadence as the melodic-harmonic crux of the passage, emphasizes it by a suspension, and omits the final melodic turn around the dominant note present in Diabelli's theme. The clipping-away of the end of the theme seems entirely appropriate for this miniature variation, the most laconic member of the set.

Ex. 10

Immediately following the Wittgenstein sketch are two attempts at a draft for Var. 19, the first skeletal, the second bearing a strong resemblance to the finished variation. In the sequences of the second of these drafts (bars 25–8), Beethoven reconciles the motivic figuration of this variation with another reharmonization of the passage (Ex. 11). This material is then literally restated one tone higher in the manner of the 'Schusterfleck' from Diabelli's theme. Beethoven subsequently copied this sketch into Landsberg 10, and used it with slight refinement in the finished piece. It is the only variation in the set which preserves these sequences of the theme, and even here Beethoven admits only two repetitions of the chromatically ascending pattern. He diverts the third repetition to the tonal stability of the tonic, while bringing back the canonic material from the opening of the variation.

Ex. 11

The draft of Var. 19 in PLM is interesting in a sense that concerns the relation between successive variations. In the draft, no cadence is provided at the end. It resolves instead to a dramatic interruption, prior to the beginning of the Poco adagio variation, an early version of the mysterious Var. 20 of the finished work (Ex. 12). The following draft for Var. 21, moreover, is connected by an incomplete cadence to the beginning of the variation 'alla don giovanni' that succeeds it (Ex. 13).

Ex. 12

Ex. 13

These examples show in the most striking way how concerned Beethoven was to maintain a thread between even these most diversified variations of the work. In the end, he resolved not to connect these variations by means of over-lapping cadences, although he did utilize that technique to enforce continuity between the last slow variation and the Fugue in E flat, and between the Fugue and the closing Minuet. Of course, within the smaller dimensions of the work as it was planned in 1819, the interconnected variations were indeed located toward the end of the piece, and the plan to couple such diversified variations may have been a response to the drastic contrasts embodied by their juxtaposition. Beethoven may well have felt a need to impose control over the internal momentum of the work so as to prepare for its conclusion. In the finished work, he took great pains to re-establish a sense of large formal stability in the closing variations, and this led him to important innovations in form not yet evident in the plans from 1819. This problem will be taken up again later in conjunction with the structure of the completed work.

A comparison of the early plan for the Diabelli Variations with the finished work is shown in Table 3. It will be seen that when Beethoven took up his draft into the final version he left the order of variations unchanged, and expanded the work mainly from within. The framework for the whole was already nearly complete in the draft, for the penultimate 'minore' variation and the beginning of the Fugue were included. We have even observed that material related to some variations composed only later—such as Vars. 1 and 15—can also be discerned in the early sketches. The problem of finding a satisfactory musical and emotional progression also seems to have been a preoccupation of the composer from the beginning, for a group of variations near the beginning of the work was actually composed in order, and most of the others found their final order in the set of loose drafts from 1819. Particularly interesting is the manner in which Beethoven derives basic musical material and then appropriates it to individual variations: a network of interrelationships can exist among several variations which explore, as it were, different aspects of a central idea. Generally speaking, such interrelated variations were separated, often widely, in the variation order.

Another illustration of this practice is provided by a sketch found in slightly varied form in two sources: on the reverse of the first page of the autograph, and in Paris 77B, the bifolium separated from the Wittgenstein Sketchbook. It corresponds to bars 8–12 of the theme and introduces appoggiaturas supported by diminished harmonies, each of which resolves to a chord derived from the theme (Ex. 14). This short sketch is analysed most fruitfully in conjunction with a draft for a prototype of Var. 21 which appears two pages later in Wittgenstein (Paris 77B). This draft lacks the distinctive alternation of duple and triple metre familiar to us from the finished variation, and uses material in its sequential bars that was ultimately destined not for Var. 21 at all, but for another variation in duple metre, the march, No. 16. The march

Ex. 14

TABLE 3. A comparison of the early plan for the
Diabelli Variations with the finished work

Draft (1819)	Finished Work (1823)
	1*†
	2†
1	3
2	4
3‡	5
4‡	6
5‡	7
6‡	8
7	9
8	10
9	11
10	12
11	13
12	14
	15*†
13	16
14	17
15	18
16	19
17	20
18	21
19	22
unused variation	23†
	24†
	25†
	26*†
20	27
	28*†
	29†
21 ('minore')	30
	31†
22 (Fugue)	32
	33†

* Variations absent from Draft for which related
material occurs in Wittgenstein – Paris 77B.

† Variations (11 in all) missing from 1819 Draft.

‡ Variations in missing bifolium.

variation, on the other hand, had already absorbed the above sketch material with the dissonant appoggiaturas by the time it was entered into the Landsberg 10 draft. And in the final version of Var. 16, the texture of this passage is enriched by the presence of a chromatically ascending motive modelled closely on the theme, which begins in the treble and then passes to the bass. The motif used is precisely what Beethoven had previously planned for Var. 21 (Paris 77B, fol. 2ᵛ), as Ex. 15 shows.

Ex. 15

During the late period of composition on Op. 120 Beethoven found compelling means of combining these two ideas derived from Diabelli's sequences. The ascent in chromatic semitones (bracketed in Ex. 16) is shaped into sequences spanning a third and shifting in register; the appoggiaturas outlining a fourth are treated melodically, and intensified through rhythmic diminution in bar 7. These devices contribute to the increasing excitement in the music of this passage from the final version of Var. 16 (see Ex. 16).

Ex. 16

Another variation from 1822-3, No. 28, also utilizes the idea of the aforementioned sketch from Paris 77B and p. 1 of the autograph. Now the appoggiatura on a diminished-seventh chord becomes a kind of ostinato maintained throughout; not only is the material from the sketch present in bars 8–12, but it dominates the melodic and harmonic structure in the entire first half of the variation. The very first bar of the final version of Var. 28 contains this .progression, transposed from the dominant to the tonic (see Ex. 17). This material of course lends itself well to the kind of drastic fore-shortening accomplished in Var. 28 (see p. 113), and its treatment here contrasts sharply with that in Var. 16 or in the other variations that ultimately utilize this material, Nos. 2 and 3. In the Paris 77A draft of Var. 3, this characteristic motive is not yet evident, and indeed it could not be used without adaptation, since it is sketched in duple metre, whereas Var. 3 was always conceived in triple metre. Beethoven, however, subsequently succeeded in adapting this material by utilizing a technique which pre-occupied him intensely, to judge from the evidence of the sketches: the technique of syncopation.

Ex. 17

One sketch for these sequential bars, syncopated throughout, recurs so often in the early sketch sources that it deserves detailed attention. It occurs in whole or in part five times in the various documents. The form of the sketch from p. 1 of the autograph, on the reverse of the leaf containing Beethoven's copy of Diabelli's theme, is shown in Ex. 18. This same sketch, as the con-tinuation of an unused variation that was to have been syncopated through-out, occurs in Wittgenstein, fol. 7ʳ, and in a later layer of Paris 58B, fol. 1ᵛ.

Ex. 18

Subsequently, the part of this sketch occupied by the syncopated sequences was attached by Beethoven to Var. 21 (see Ex. 19). This version, from the Landsberg 10 draft, p. 174, is the first appearance in Beethoven's sketches of

Ex. 19

the contrast between 4/4 and 3/4 metre familiar from the finished work.[21] In all probability, this draft represents a tentative solution that Beethoven found unsatisfactory, for in the second half he utilizes still another 3/4 sketch, also found in several sources, to couple with the opening material.

His final solution was based on this second 3/4 sketch, but the concept represented in the first was exploited in his final revisions of the third variation, and in the composition of the second variation. Both of these late-composed variations bring identical harmonies to bars 9-12, and in both harmonic changes occur on the second or third beats of the bar, while the diminished harmonies from the sequence are sustained through the first beat of each bar by repeated sonorities and, in Var. 3, by tied notes. These two variations at the beginning of the set are thus heir to Beethoven's intense preoccupation with syncopation and to his concern, also illustrated by Vars. 16 and 28, to heighten the musical tension of these sequences by means of dissonant secondary harmonies and appoggiaturas.

Thus in the case of Var. 3, as with No. 16, Beethoven found a means of combining two concept sketches together in the finished work. In both, this synthesis was first achieved after extensive sketching had been done, and the variations had attained a fairly advanced stage in composition. Meanwhile, other variations, though sharing common material, were developed with such verve and consistency that their individuality is in no way impaired by the kinship. Indeed, it seems that Beethoven's compositional method frequently involved the shaping of material for different variations from a common mould of musical relationships, and a study of the sketches reveals numerous

[21] The fifth, abbreviated appearance of this material is in Artaria 180/200, pp. 35-6 (DS, East Berlin), which contains only two bars. This sketch was evidently a momentary continuation of Landsberg 10, p. 174, a sheet to which Beethoven resorted when he made a mistake at the top of Landsberg 10, p. 175. After sketching only these two bars Beethoven returned to Landsberg 10 for the continuation.

points of contact in the evolution of the variations, including many that are not so evident from the finished work.

Examples of such affinities between variations in the Wittgenstein Sketchbook exist in abundance, and still more could be cited. The first part of Var. 5 in the sketches is interconnected with the first part of the ninteenth; the strange harmonies in the sequential bars of the twentieth variation bear some relation with the corresponding passage in Var. 15. Other variations, such as No. 11, parallel, to a degree, several different variations with which they share material and techniques. In view of this pervasive network of relationships linking the many members of the set, it is not surprising that most of Beethoven's advanced work on these variations seems to have been directed towards imparting and perfecting an individuality of conception and sentiment. Often this process resulted in the de-emphasis, and sometimes even the obliteration, of shared features.

PLANS FOR THE CLOSING VARIATIONS (VARS. 26, 27, 30, 32)

We have not yet discussed Beethoven's early sketches and drafts for the later variations of the set, which are particularly interesting in view of the profound changes that this part of the work was to undergo in the second period of composition on Op. 120. The fragment of the end of the draft preserved by the Montauban leaf shows a 'presto', which entered the finished work as Var. 27; a 'minore', an early version of Var. 30; and the theme and counter-subject of the penultimate E flat Fugue. In the early draft, then, Var. 27, instead of forming a group with its contiguous neighbours, stood alone, and was followed directly by the 'minore', Var. 30. This is the only one of the slow minor variations found in the early sketches and drafts.

Var. 27 was already quite advanced in composition in 1819, if we can judge from the three bars, near its close, preserved in Montauban (see Ex. 20). The Wittgenstein Sketchbook contains little material, however, to document the evolution of this variation. This touches upon a rather surprising disparity between the Draft and sketchbook; for whereas a draft for most of the first half of Var. 26 exists in Wittgenstein (Paris 77B), this variation is absent from the PLM Draft. Nevertheless, these two variations are best treated together, because of their close musical kinship. In the finished work, Beethoven paired them together as part of a larger group of four, Vars. 25–8.

Ex. 20

The sketch for Var. 26 was made after the adjacent entries in Paris 77B, and its later origin is reflected by the differing shades of ink. Cramped for space to write, since most of the page had been filled with earlier sketches, he continued his sketch onto the bottom of the same page (Paris 77B fol. 1ʳ) and then to the following page in pencil, showing the connection by 'vi–de' signs. These fragments are assembled in Ex. 21. Beethoven also added a number to this draft, '15', on fol. 1ʳ, and at the end of the draft, he scrawled the notation 'Hiernach Marsch' in large letters. These intriguing references to the variation order of the burgeoning set deserve detailed attention, because they line up with a system of numbers written in pencil, and placed before several variations in Wittgenstein. These are shown in Table 4. These numbers seem to represent a provisional order of variations that Beethoven considered while sketching in Wittgenstein, and then rejected by the time the corresponding entries were made in the Draft. As we have seen, Beethoven had followed the order of his incipits in Paris 58B in developing the first few variations of his Draft, Vars. 3-7. Subsequently, after Var. 7, most of the variations seem to

Ex. 21   Paris 77B MS fol. 1ʳ (top)

fol. 1ʳ (bottom)   fol. 1v (top)

TABLE 4. Provisional order of variations in the Wittgenstein sketchbook

Numbering in Wittgenstein Sketchbook	Numbering in final version
'11'	11
'12'	unused
'13'	19
'14'	8
'15'	26
[16] (these variation numbers	16
[17] (implied by 'Hiernach Marsch')	17

have taken shape before their order was determined: Var. 8, for instance, is labelled '14', in a sequence that bears little resemblance to the finished work.

It is interesting that Beethoven contemplated placing Var. 26 before No. 16, identified by him as 'Ma[rsch]' in Wittgenstein, since one of his last additions to the set was to insert the Presto scherzando into this position in the order. On the surface, this might even seem to imply a late origin for the sketch, which could have been made in 1823, when Beethoven doubtless scrutinized his earlier sketches. This is unlikely, however. It would be surprising if Beethoven had considered separating Vars. 26–7 at that stage, since they are so closely related. More likely is that the Wittgenstein sketch was actually a preliminary study for the draft of Var. 27 in Montauban; and this may account for the lack of sketches for Var. 27 in the sketchbook.

On the other hand, an abundance of material exists for the 'minore' matrix. The first sketch for it, on fol. 6^r, is among the most visionary of the many revealing sketches contained in Wittgenstein (see Ex. 22). This is clearly a precursor of the 'minore' contained in Montauban, in which the melodic sequence and descent from A flat is still harmonized to lead to the dominant, following the theme. Already in Montauban, this second phrase settles in the Neapolitan, D flat, a solution retained in the final version. The bass line in the Wittgenstein sketch, with its fall and ascent of the thematic fourth, C–G, is only slightly changed in the draft, and imitative entries in four voices are added (see Ex. 23).

Ex. 22

Ex. 23

In the Montauban draft for this variation, the proportions between parts of the variation follow the theme, although only half as many bars are required. (The first eight bars of the theme correspond to the first four bars in Var. 30, and in both cases this represents half of the first section of the variation.) However, in several of the last variations composed in 1822–3—in Vars. 29, 33, and especially 31—Beethoven alters these proportions. This development, which represents a major innovation of the Diabelli Variations, seems to be indistinctly foreshadowed by the above sketch from Wittgenstein.

Unlike the Montauban draft, which moves in slow eighth notes, the Wittgenstein sketch proceeds in quarter notes, and is not extended by any kind of polyphonic imitation. The Wittengenstein sketch is, then, a fore-shortened compression of the first eight bars of Diabelli's theme, and it is almost inconceivable that these proportions, with this kind of movement, could be maintained throughout an entire slow variation. Some kind of expansion or extension would be needed. One solution was to maintain the proportions of the theme by means of an internal, polyphonic expansion of the opening bars, as in Montauban Var. 30. Another solution was to foreshorten the harmonically static beginning of Diabelli's theme, while expanding the rest, which can be enlivened by harmonic movement and the development of material from the opening of the variation. This short sketch, suggestive in its rhythmic and melodic contour of features of the great thirty-first variation, provides some hint of the formal innovations that characterize Beethoven's most far-reaching transformation of Diabelli's waltz.

It is noteworthy that Var. 30, as drafted in Montauban, had a regular struc-ture with both halves repeated. Beethoven eventually excised the repetition from the first half, and reduced the repetition in the second half to only the last four bars. One reason for these changes may be the intimate, continuous bond formed in the final version by this trio of slow variations, which together represent a kind of composite slow movement for the entire cycle. Another factor is probably the fact that both of the other slow variations in the minor show great freedom in their proportional relationship to the theme, so that Var. 30, by contrast, seems starkly regular; this regularity is rendered less obvious by the omission of repetitions and reiteration of the last four bars in the finished work. Finally, overall length may also have been a factor, especially in view of the great length of the ornate Largo, Var. 31.

But in any case, Var. 31, clearly one of the last variations to be conceived, plays no role in Beethoven's plans for the set from 1819. This is confirmed by the sketches at the end of Var. 30 on the Montauban leaf for what appears to be a transition from this minor variation to the Fugue in E flat (see the transcription in Part III, Fig. 21).

The fugue theme and countersubject already contain many essential features of the finished work, including the descending sequences in the countersubject (see Ex. 24). Only four bars of this draft survive at the end of the fragment; but fortunately we possess some further sketches for the Fugue in Wittgenstein. These were evidently among the last sketches for Op. 120 made by Beethoven in 1819, for they appear four pages into the work on the Mass, on fol. 11^r, juxtaposed with entries for the Credo. At this stage, it appears, Beethoven reversed his general practice of working first in the

Ex. 24

sketchbook, and afterwards in the Draft. These Wittgenstein sketches—four in all—deal with the working-out of contrapuntal material, and they omit but presuppose the form of the subject which appears in Montauban. The first of these sketches is shown in Ex. 25, together with the fugue subject from the Draft. These sketches imply that the 1819 Draft contained more material for the fugue, now lost. Nevertheless, it seems unlikely, in view of later sketches, that Beethoven carried through this work for the fugue very far in the Draft. The fugue subject and countersubject are still not in their final form in the Engelmann Sketchbook, from the spring of 1823, and a considerable number of changes in the fugue took place as late as the writing of the autograph. It would indeed be interesting to know if Beethoven had sketched a finale or recapitulation after the fugue, but the continuation of this Draft, if it existed, is now lost. The first sketches for the Minuet finale are found in the Paris 96 MS from 1823; no sketches for it are evident in Wittgenstein.

Ex. 25

[Montauban Subject]

The answer to the problem of the finale resides with two sketches in Wittgenstein: one juxtaposed with the above fugal sketch, and another found in Paris 77B, fol. 2ʳ. The latter idea is faint, and scarcely legible. Beginning as a single-voice sketch for the bass of the 'minore', Var. 30, it continues as a transition passage leading to a 'presto' modelled on the theme and most probably in G major. This is connected to a statement of Diabelli's theme in 3/8 metre with an accompaniment in sixteenth notes (see Ex. 26). This sketch offers formidable difficulties in transcription, and should be regarded with a measure of critical reserve. Yet it does suggest a convincing solution to the riddle of the finale, if we read the 'presto' in G major and the 'all[egr]o molto' in C major, as is implied by the notation 'ganzes Thema'. This suggests that Beethoven considered closing the work with a Ländler transformation of the

Ex. 26

waltz following the slow variation in the minor. Evidently, when he ventured this sketch, Beethoven had not yet settled on the idea of a fugue in penultimate position.

This is an amazing throwback in style, suggesting the modulating Ländler type of variation coda such as Beethoven employed in some of his early piano variations of the 1790s. One is also reminded of his early Quartet in B flat, Op. 18 No. 6, in which the poignant slow introduction 'La Malinconia' passes into a finale invested with the spirit of the Viennese ballrooms.[22] If so, the change in course which led to the Minuet finale of 1823 is even more impressive, contrasted with these jejune beginnings.

The later sketch, on fol. 11ʳ in Wittgenstein, contains a transition from the E flat Fugue to the finale, anticipating in a striking way the miraculous transition of the finished work, particularly the emphasis on the diminished-seventh chord supporting C flat (Ex. 27). Following a pause on the dominant

Ex. 27

[22] Cf. Kerman's discussion of Op. 18, No. 6 in *The Beethoven Quartets*, pp. 75–82.

seventh of C, Beethoven writes what appears to be the beginning of a melodic subject close to Diabelli's theme. The retrospective Paris 77B sketch is thus superseded here by plans for a penultimate Fugue in E flat, culminating in a dramatic transition modulating back to C. A finale, however, is all but lacking. Beethoven had to wait several years—until after the completion of his last piano sonata—before he would discover the optimal solution for a finale to Op. 120.

At this point, with drafts or notes on paper for approximately twenty-four variations, Beethoven turned his energy to what was probably the greatest single compositional obsession of his career, the *Missa Solemnis*. Beethoven hoped to finish the Mass in time for the elevation of the Archduke Rudolph to Archbishop in March of 1820, and pressure to finish this score, as well as the uncommon force (related in several contemporary accounts) with which the composition of the Mass gripped him, may account for the fact that the Variations were put aside. They were not to be revived until the very end of 1822, after completion of the Mass in all but a few details.

Nor was Beethoven in any particular hurry to sell the Variations to a publisher. After the aforementioned letter from February, 1820, there is no reference to Op. 120 in Beethoven's extant correspondence until the spring of 1822, although Beethoven was in frequent contact with several publishers to whom he might have offered the Variations. Finally, in a letter to Peters in Leipzig, from 5 June 1822, Beethoven mentions 'Variations on a waltz for pianoforte solo (there are many variations)'.[23] And a few months later, in November 1822, the composer writes to Anton Diabelli himself in more explicit terms: 'The fee for the variations would be 40 ducats at most, provided they are worked out on as large a scale as is planned. But if this does not materialize, then I would quote a smaller fee.'[24] In Beethoven's own words, '... im Falle sie so groß ausgeführt werden als die Anlage davon ist; sollte dies aber nicht statthaben ...' As Beethoven himself implies in this letter, the 'Anlage', or plan for the variations, was large; and it included all of the sources that we have thus far discussed.

We shall now turn to the late period of work on Op. 120, which began at about the time that this written offer to Diabelli was made. Beethoven added at the end of this letter to Diabelli: 'Kindly let me have a reply about my offer—I hope to be able to make a start on your variations before the end of next week.' According to the evidence of the sketchbooks as analysed by Robert Winter,[25] this new 'start' on an old work did indeed take place around November 1822.

[23] Anderson, L. 1079. Anderson mistranslates 'viele' as 'several' instead of 'many'.
[24] Anderson, L. 1105.
[25] See Winter's discussion of the chronology of the Artaria 201 Sketchbook in *The Beethoven Sketchbooks*.

III. The Late Sketches (1822–3)

INTRODUCTION

The basic chronicle of Beethoven's compositional activity in the year 1822 is the Artaria 201 Sketchbook. This sketchbook begins with work on the Piano Sonata, Op. 111, which was finished early in the year, continues with late sketches for the Agnus of the Mass, and then records work on the Overture in C, Op. 124, which was completed by early autumn.[1] In its present last pages are found sketches for the Diabelli Variations—the first sketches for the work since the Wittgenstein Sketchbook and contemporaneous drafts were used, three-and-a-half years before.

The unique chronological position of these entries may help explain their otherwise somewhat puzzling content. Unlike the sketches in Wittgenstein, most of which directly entered the fabric of the work, the sketches in Artaria 201 have a tentative, searching quality about them, and were not, for the most part, taken into the work at all. There are sketches for the Fugue, Var. 32, as well as for Vars. 3, 10, and for an unused variation bearing some resemblance to Vars. 26 and 27.

These sketches directly follow a series of incipits for all movements of the Ninth Symphony, Op. 125, on p. 123, and are the first instance of juxtaposition of sketches for Op. 120 and Op. 125 that also occurs in the other three major surviving sources for late Variation sketches; the Paris MSS 57 and 96 and the Engelmann Sketchbook. In all of these cases Beethoven turned to the first movement of the Ninth Symphony after working on the Variations,[2] and after the completion of Op. 120 by the end of April 1823, it was the Ninth Symphony that preoccupied Beethoven for the remainder of that year. The Variations were thus conceived at about the same time as work began on the Kyrie of the Mass, and brought to completion just before Beethoven's most intense period of composition on the Ninth Symphony. An outline of this chronology is shown in Table 5.

As this chronology shows, the composition of the Diabelli Variations straddles practically the entire evolution of the *Missa Solemnis*. It is striking

---

[1] It was performed 3 October 1822. The autograph is dated 'am Ende September'.
[2] Nottebohm's observation that Beethoven worked on Op. 120 with interruptions, usually turning to the first movement of the Ninth Symphony, is correct as far as the late sketches for Op. 120 are concerned. See Nottebohm, p. 572.

TABLE 5. The chronology of Op. 120 relative to other works of 1819–23

Date	Sketchbook	Work	Summary
1819	Wittgenstein	Op. 120	Diabelli Variations
		Op. 123	begun
1820		Op. 109 (?)	Sustained work on
			Mass begun
	Artaria 195	Op. 123, Credo	
		Op. 109	
		Op. 119	
		Op. 123, Benedictus	
1821	Artaria 197	Op. 123, Agnus	
		Dona	
		Op. 110	
1822	Artaria 201	Op. 111	Sustained work on
		Op. 123, Agnus	Mass finished
		Op. 124	
		Op. 120	
1823	Engelmann	Op. 120	Diabelli Variations
		Op. 125	completed
			Sustained work on
			Ninth Symphony begun
	Landsberg 8	Op. 125	

that although Beethoven interrupted work on the Mass for the composition of the last piano sonatas, the sketchbooks preserve no evidence of an awakened interest in the Variations during these years. Yet the last movement of the last sonata, the famous Arietta of Op. 111, displays a complex interrelationship with Op. 120. The theme of this variation movement shows an obvious indebtedness to Op. 120, as Jürgen Uhde has carefully pointed out,[3] and the sketches for this work show,[4] moreover, that the final version of the theme was attained only after much sustained labour on the movement. In turn, the entire last variation and coda of Op. 120 show a profound debt to the Arietta, a relationship much more extensive than the near quotation of the falling fourth cited by Charles Rosen in *The Classical Style*.[5] We shall have occasion to examine this relationship more closely in connection with the sketches for the end of Op. 120 preserved in the Engelmann Sketchbook, and again when we

[3] *Beethovens Klaviermusik*, vol. I (Stuttgart, 1968), pp. 504–6.
[4] For a transcription of these sketches, see vol. II of William Drabkin's unpublished Ph.D. dissertation, *A Study of Beethoven's Opus 111 and its Sources* (Princeton, 1977).
[5] p. 445.

inquire into the musical substance of the finished work (see below pp. 115–18, 126–30).

Unlike the early work on Op. 120, most of which seems to have been preserved, even if widely dispersed, the later sketches are obviously incomplete. No sketches survive for Vars. 1, 24, 25, and 31,[6] and some of these, particularly the Fughetta and the last slow variation, must have demanded extensive preliminary work. It is of course true that Beethoven in general, and particularly the ageing Beethoven, did extensive composition in the autographs of many compositions. The autographs of the Kyrie of the Mass in D and the last movement of the Piano Sonata, Op. 110 are outstanding examples of this phenomenon, in which the distinction between autograph and sketch is itself called into question.[7] And while the autograph of Op. 120 begins as a very clean copy, its later pages are increasingly filled with revisions and corrections. One passage, the transition from the thirty-first variation to the Fugue, is actually left incomplete in the autograph. Still, the five basic extant sketch sources—Artaria 201, Paris 57, Paris 96, the Engelmann Sketchbook, and the autograph itself—probably preserve less than half of the late sketches for the Diabelli Variations.

There is reason to believe that a group of sketches from the winter of 1822–3 has been lost. This is suggested not only by the paucity of Op. 120 sketches, but also by that of preliminary material for several other contemporary works. Some sketches for the first movement of the Ninth Symphony are probably missing, although exact assessment of the loss still awaits thorough study of the material. Other sketches seem to be missing for the 'Opferlied', Op. 121b, the 'Bundeslied', Op. 122, and for the revised version of the first six Bagatelles from Op. 119.[8] Some of these sketches might once have been placed at the beginning of the Engelmann Sketchbook, which is undersized, implying that it may have been dismantled after Beethoven's death. In any case, clarification of the chronology of Beethoven's late work on the Variations requires study of the complex relationship between two principal sources for Ninth Symphony sketches: the Engelmann Sketchbook, and the two bundles of Landsberg 8, now housed in East Berlin.

Robert Winter has pointed out that Paris 96, a gathered sheet containing three pages of sketches for the Variations followed by Ninth Symphony sketches, belongs, in all probability, at the beginning of the first bundle of Landsberg 8.[9] Manuscript 96 shares the same paper type, gathering structure,

[6] As we have seen, for Var. 1 there does exist some related material in Wittgenstein, which is not true for the others.

[7] See Lewis Lockwood, 'On Beethoven's Sketches and Autographs: Some Problems of Definition and Interpretation', *Acta musicologica*, xiii (1970), pp. 32–47.

[8] This was pointed out to me by Sieghard Brandenburg, at the Beethoven-Archiv in Bonn.

[9] Winter, *The Beethoven Sketchbooks*. This reconstruction is also provided in Winter's article 'The Sketches for the "Ode to Joy" ', in *Beethoven, Performers, and Critics. The International Beethoven Congress, Detroit, 1977*, ed. R. Winter and B. Carr (Detroit, 1980), p. 210.

and stab holes with Landsberg 8, and Winter's placement of this gathered sheet at the head of the first bundle of Ninth Symphony sketches is convincing. As Winter himself points out, however, this implies that these fugue sketches for Op. 120 were made before Beethoven began to use this bundle continuously for work on Op. 125, for the Landsberg 8 sketches are all more advanced than corresponding sketches for the Ninth Symphony in Engelmann, whereas for Op. 120 the reverse is true. Paris 96 contains preliminary sketches for the Fugue, which seem earlier than the corresponding entries in Engelmann.

The picture is further complicated, moreover, by a layer of pencil corrections in Paris 96 that cannot have occurred before the work in Engelmann. It seems that sometime after Beethoven wrote the sketches in Paris 96 and had begun work on Op. 120 in Engelmann he returned to Paris 96 and made revisions and additions in pencil. He then returned to Engelmann, and finished sketching the Variations in that sketchbook. Even after the autograph was written out, Beethoven returned to Engelmann to write out a clean copy of Diabelli's waltz for his copyist,[10] and to make extensive corrections for the *Abschrift* sent to Ferdinand Ries in London. Subsequently he filled the remainder of the Engelmann Sketchbook with work on the Ninth Symphony, and then went back once again to continue sketching the symphony in Landsberg 8, which was, up to that point, practically unused. The broad outlines of this complicated chronological sequence are indicated in Fig. 4. Adding to the complications attending these sources is the likelihood, recently pointed out by Brandenberg, that the entire complex—Engelmann, Paris 96 and the first bundle of Landsberg 8—was bound together at some point by Beethoven as a single sketchbook, 'Sketchbook K' in the later Artaria classification.[11]

It is hazardous to speculate about the date of the entries in Paris 96 because of the lack of other Op. 120 sketches that may have preceded or followed them. Anton Schindler's statement that Beethoven composed the Variations in the winter of 1822–3 must, of course, be regarded with extreme caution.[12] Nevertheless, although no extant sketches for Op. 120 can be shown to date from the winter of 1822–3, it is plausible that Paris 96 and other lost sketches stem from this period. From the evidence of Beethoven's letter to Diabelli and his sketches at the end of Artaria 201, he seems to have revived composition of Op. 120 by the late autumn of 1822; on the other side we know that the Variations were finished by the end of April, since the *Abschrift* sent to Ries

[10] This was not Rampl, as has been claimed in the literature, but copyist E, in the nomenclature devised by Alan Tyson. See Tyson, 'Notes on Five of Beethoven's Copyists', *Journal of the American Musicological Association*, xxiii (1970), pp. 460–3.

[11] A reconstruction of these and other related sources is provided in Brandenburg, 'Die Skizzen zur Neunten Symphonie', *Zu Beethoven: Aufsätze und Dokumente*, ii, ed. H. Goldschmidt (Berlin, 1984), pp. 115–20.

[12] Schindler, pp. 221–2.

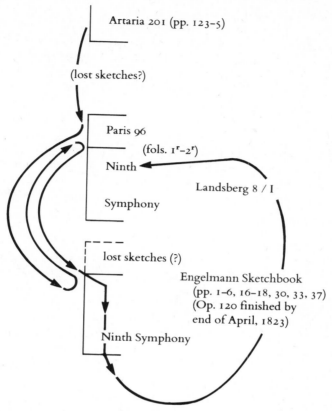

Fig. 4. Chronological sequence of the principal sources for the late sketches of Op. 120.

bears the inscription 'am 30ten April'. Two other pieces of documentary evidence deserve attention here: in a letter to Schindler, dated by Anderson as from January 1823, Beethoven writes: 'I see from my notebook that you have doubts about that business with Diab[elli] concerning the Mass. So I beg you to come soon. In that case we will not give him the var[iations] either, for my brother knows someone who will take both works.'[13] An attempt by Beethoven to sell the Variations to another publisher is borne out by a letter to Antonio Pacini in Paris, dated April 5, 1823: 'tout ce que je suis en état de vous offrir pour le coup ce sont 33 variations sur le thème d'une valse pour le piano grand oeuvre'.[14] On the basis of these documents, and the lack of sketches for

[13] Anderson, L. 1131.
[14] Anderson, L. 1166.

several other works, it is a reasonable conjecture that Variation sketches from the early part of the year 1823 have disappeared. To judge from their preliminary and experimental quality, the fugal sketches in Paris 96 most probably preceded the majority of the lost sketches for the Diabelli Variations, and stem from the first months of 1823. With this broad outline before us, we can turn to the more palpable evidence from Beethoven's sketchbooks.

ARTARIA 201 (VARS. 3, 10)

Among the Artaria 201 sketches is a draft for Var. 3 which differs considerably from the draft in Paris 77A. The descent from E to G, worked out in the latter manuscript and retained in the autograph, is lacking here, and the opening phrase remains anchored to the pitch level of the opening note, C (Ex. 28). The remainder of this variation makes extensive use of the rhythmic motive ♩♪ | ♩

, which is exploited in only one of the finished variations, No. 5. In the end, however, Beethoven rejected this sketch for the finished work, and instead refined the draft of Var. 3 at the head of the Paris 77A manuscript. The development of Beethoven's compositional ideas did not always follow a straight line, a fact that has often emerged from close studies of his sketches. It seems, in fact, that Beethoven at first had difficulty finding his way back into the world of the Variations. Having set the work aside for so long, the internal musical context of the composition was no longer alive in him.

Ex. 28

An analogous case is presented by a sketch for the beginning of Var. 10 on p. 123 of Artaria (Ex. 29). Here the descending scale in the bass is coupled with an ascending figure in broken sixths which forms a scale rising in contrary motion with the bass. In the finished work, Beethoven discarded the idea of the ascending sixths in the treble and returned to the bass theme alone (with upbeat, also omitted in Artaria 201), relocating the upper part to the role of a stationary pedal. He had already hit on this solution in Wittgenstein. The Artaria 201 sketch for this variation probably records an attempt to fill out the conception recorded in the Paris-Landsberg draft, where the first bars are missing in the treble. But like the Artaria sketch for the third variation, it found no place in the autograph.

Ex. 29

Another sketch, faint and scarcely legible, provides a single treble line in continuous eighth notes in compound metre, with material akin to that used in Vars. 26 and 27. The chromatic inflections and repetition of figures resembles No. 27, while the rhythm and metre are close to those used in No. 26. These bars possibly correspond to the sequences in the second part of the first half of the theme. But if Beethoven contemplated a variation using this material, it did not surface in the final version. The Artaria sketch is shown in Ex. 30.

Ex. 30

Perhaps the most interesting sketch in Artaria 201 preserves an attempt to compose the transition from the Fugue in E flat to the Finale (see Ex. 31). This was to have involved a momentous pause on an E flat octave, followed by a sudden, unprepared shift to the dominant of C, affirmed by the urgent intensity of Beethoven's fugue subject. This led, in turn, into a 9/8 finale, of which, unfortunately, precious little was notated. This sketch contains little of the wonderful harmonic subtlety of the passage in the finished work. It even

Ex. 31

lacks the harmonic progression of the early Wittgenstein sketch, which was ultimately utilized by Beethoven. Other key features, however, are in evidence. The E♭–G progression of the sketch foreshadows the bass movement of this passage in the completed work, and the high register of the Finale is already part of Beethoven's sketch. The transition in Artaria 201, in spite of the effectiveness of its dramatic contrasts, is infinitely inferior to the modulation later devised by Beethoven, but at the same time, it bears seeds that were later to come to fruition.

The fragment of the finale sketched is fascinating, though at first glance it might seem incoherent. This sketch presents a decorated form of the upbeat from the waltz, with the melody then doubled at the tenth. The sixteenth-note pattern in 9/8 metre is reminiscent of the fourth variation of the Arietta movement of Op. 111 which, as we shall see, later became a compositional model for the coda of Op. 120. The end of this brief sketch, on the other hand, foreshadows the striking syncopated close of the finished work. Here, as elsewhere in Beethoven's compositional process, the characteristic rhythmic framework seems to have come into being before the composer determined the shape of his thematic material.

Paris 96 (Vars. 32, 33)

The next surviving sketches for the Diabelli Variations, preserved in the Paris 96 manuscript, are mainly confined to the Fugue, with one notable exception. This manuscript contains the first surviving reference to the final Minuet variation, and the sketch is so entitled by Beethoven (see Ex. 32). This sketch already contains the opening motif from the final version (reminiscent of the beginning of the Arietta from Op. 111), an idea that here also plays a role in the second part of the first variation half. Repetition of the figure at this place was later suppressed by Beethoven, despite the importance of this motif. In the first part of this sketch, on the other hand, everything is retained, to be later enhanced by ornamentation. It is noteworthy that in this sketch Beethoven foreshortens the harmonically static opening bars of Diabelli's theme; manipulation of the period structure of the theme, a resource Beethoven used to great effect in several of the last variations, makes here its first unequivocal appearance in the sketchbooks. The first four bars of the theme are condensed into two, while the following bars, which seem to correspond to Diabelli's sequences, still correspond to the structure of the

Ex. 32

Letzte Menu[et]

theme, bar by bar. Beethoven could thereby modify the formal stiffness of Diabelli's model, and open up possibilities for increasing continuity and freedom of conception exploited to the utmost in the last slow minor variation.

In his essay on the sketches for Op. 120, Nottebohm quoted liberally from the fugue sketches in Paris 96, and concluded that the Variations were, by this time, close to completion. However, it is by no means clear that these sketches were among his last before Beethoven began the autograph. Nottebohm fails to mention the presence of two layers of writing in Paris 96. Most of the sketches were made in the same shade of ink, but some revisions and further sketches were made in pencil. Evidence of a temporal gap between these entries is unmistakable; most of the ink sketches are attempts to refine the principal countersubject of the Fugue, and to find a second countersubject in running eighth notes. It appears, therefore, that Beethoven may already have premeditated a triple fugue at this stage, or at least a fugue with two distinct countersubjects. Beethoven also made sketches for different forms of augmentation of the theme, in combination with the running countersubject. But in the end, no such augmentation was applied to the theme, and neither of the countersubjects—nor, for that matter, even the Fugue theme itself—reach their final form in this layer of sketches.

There is an experimental quality to most of these sketches; clearly the fugue and the Minuet finale had not yet taken definite shape in the composer's mind. One sketch (Ex. 33) even shows the fugue subject and running counter-subject in 3/4 time—quite a departure from the duple metre of the other sketches and of the final version. Another sketch (Ex. 34) presents the transition from the Fugue to the Minuet as a long, sustained trill circling over the dominant of C major. Yet, despite their tentative nature, the sketches in

Ex. 33

Ex. 34

Paris 96 preserve an important stage in the evolution of the Fugue. The notion of combining the fugue subject with two other contrasting subjects is first manifest in Paris 96. When Beethoven returned at a later time to revise his ideas in this manuscript, he arrived at once at forms of the fugue subject and countersubject which were taken, almost without change, into the final version.

However, as we have already remarked, before Beethoven made these revisions in Paris 96, he seems to have made at least some of the sketches in the Engelmann Sketchbook. The fugue subject and countersubject from Engelmann are shown in Ex. 35. But the last refinement in the countersubject—the use of a whole note G in the second bar rather than two half notes G–F—appears in a pencil sketch on the first page of Paris 96 (Ex. 36). The ink

Ex. 35

Ex. 36

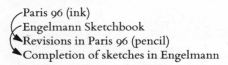

* E natural is included in a pencil revision of an adjacent sketch.

sketches for this material in Paris 96 also bear corrections in pencil that tally with the above version. This implies that the chronological sequence in composition was probably the following:

Paris 96 (ink)
Engelmann Sketchbook
Revisions in Paris 96 (pencil)
Completion of sketches in Engelmann

Unfortunately, the Engelmann Sketchbook in its present condition contains very few sketches for the fugue, and any other loose drafts for it have disappeared. The pencil revisions in Paris 96 are thus the last extant sketches for the fugue before the autograph of Op. 120. For the Minuet and coda, however, a very complete draft exists in Engelmann. This sketchbook also contains a full draft for Var. 15, which is missing from the sequence in Paris-Landsberg-Montauban, and was evidently added to the work at a very late stage in composition. Before we discuss Engelmann, however, we shall turn to still another source that preserves sketches for two variations evidently added to the piece during this late period: Nos. 2 and 23.

THE AUTOGRAPH LEAF (VARS. 2, 23)

Material for both of these variations can be found on the first leaf of the autograph containing Beethoven's copy of Diabelli's theme. It will be recalled that this theme sheet also contains early sketches identical with entries in Paris 58B and Wittgenstein. In 1823, it seems to have been pressed into use for a second time.

The fact that material for either of these variations is entirely lacking in the Wittgenstein Sketchbook or the early drafts is evidence that they stem from a later period in composition. Another indication is the difference in calligraphy between the 1819 sketches and the later additions; this is particularly clear on the reverse of the leaf, where the older sketches occupy the first four systems, with the draft for Var. 23 written directly beneath them in ink of a different texture (see Plate II and the transcription in Part III, Fig. 2). The draft for Var. 2 is more complete than that for Var. 23, but much less legible, since Beethoven wrote it on spare staves under Diabelli's theme itself, and later tried to obliterate it with ink. Nevertheless, it is still possible to transcribe most of this sketch for the second variation (see Plate I and the transcription in Part III, Fig. 1). It is noteworthy that Beethoven sketched this variation so that, when space permitted, each bar of the variation was placed directly beneath the corresponding bar of the theme. It was perhaps in the interest of rendering this page with the theme less confusing for a copyist that Beethoven later tried to obliterate the sketch. If so, he failed in his objective—the leaf still proved too hard to read, and Beethoven had to copy out the theme again on an empty page of the Engelmann Sketchbook.

Both of these sketches for Vars. 2 and 23 are rough and incomplete, and it is likely that material for them, as well as for Vars. 1, 24-6, 28, 31, and 32, was contained in papers that have not survived—possibly at the beginning of the Engelmann Sketchbook. In any case, we lack detailed information about the evolution of many of the variations late in conception.

PARIS 57 (VARS. 18, 29)

Fortunately, this generalization does not hold for the first of the slow variations in the minor, Var. 29, for which work survives in the Paris 57 manuscript. The first page of Paris 57 contains a full draft of the variation, sketched at full length. In broad outline and structure, this draft closely resembles the finished variation, although it differs from it in numerous compositional details. Following this draft, the manuscript continues with sketches for the first movement of the Ninth Symphony. Two pages later, on fol. 2^r, brief entries for Var. 18 are found amid sketches for Op. 125. Like Paris 96 and the Engelmann Sketchbook, Paris 57 juxtaposes material for

Op. 120 with work on the symphony, which dominated Beethoven's compositional activities after completion of the Variations. On the basis of this evidence, the manuscript can be ascribed to early 1823.

Another piece of internal evidence confirms this dating of the Paris 57 draft. At the beginning of the draft, Beethoven has written '28', which shows that at the time the draft was made, one of the preceding variations present in the final order had not yet been added to the work. This missing variation may have been Var. 15, which is drafted in Engelmann, amid proof corrections for the finished opus.

THE ENGELMANN SKETCHBOOK (VARS. 32, 33)

Considerable material survives in Engelmann for the Minuet and coda. The most striking fact about the Minuet draft in Engelmann is that it so closely approximates to the finished work. It might seem from this that like Vars. 18 and 22, which approach their final form already in Landsberg 10, the Minuet, once begun, did not offer Beethoven difficulties in composition. Such a conclusion is unwarranted, however, because of the probability of lost preliminary sketches. The coda, on the other hand, which begins like a thirty-fourth variation sixteen bars before the final cadence, is drafted twice in Engelmann, and deviates substantially from the finished version.

For this extraordinary passage Beethoven invoked a variant of the musical idea that made possible one of the most haunting moments in all of his music: the beginning of the repetition of the second half of Var. 4 in the Arietta of the Piano Sonata in C minor, Op. 111 (Ex. 37). Here the variation has modulated

Ex. 37

to A minor, and in the high upper register, unsupported by its harmonic bass of A, the upper line traces arabesques of sound around high C, a minor sixth above the ostinato on E. The ethereal resonance of this music is created partly by its harmonic suspension—the minor sixth E–C above its unsounded bass on A—and partly by its temporal suspension, without rhythmic accent and harmonic movement. The line of thirty-second notes is perceived as a kind of motionless pulsation, strangely devoid of expression yet endowed with an almost unbearable intensity.

In the coda of the Diabelli Variations, Beethoven arrives at a similar kind of intervallic suspension of sound. Here the bass, C, is supplied, and the fifth, G, is also included as part of an ostinato, A–G. The rest of the tonal content is comprised of a set of sixths which vacillate between an upper pitch of E and C on strong beats. The overall harmonic effect, however, is of a stationary pulsation of the sonority C–E–C, an octave with its major third. Ex. 38 shows Beethoven's preliminary draft of the coda in the Engelmann Sketchbook. Subsequently Beethoven revised this passage in a way that makes the quotation from Op. 111 much more striking (see Ex. 39). He altered the triplet sixteenth notes to thirty-second notes, increasing the speed of the line by interpolating the octave above the third, E, at the beginning of this passage, and extended the addition of this octave throughout the coda.[15] Moreover, he changed the sustained pedal on C to a throbbing repetition similar to that in the Arietta. This texture, and its basis in the sonorous suspension of the major third, C–E, invests the fundamental substance of the coda (Ex. 39).

Ex. 38

Ex. 39

The draft for the coda in the Engelmann Sketchbook shows one other interesting deviation from the autograph and the finished work. This concerns the use of the subdominant harmony in the ninth to twelfth bars from the final cadence. In the finished work, the music turns on the second beat of every one of these bars to the subdominant, as part of the cadential formula, I^7–IV^b–I–$II\#$ –V^7–(I) (Ex. 40). In the Engelmann Sketchbook, this softening shift to the subdominant, though it occurs in the latter two bars, is missing from the first two (Ex. 41). A principal reason for this change has surely to do with the linear-motivic underpinning of the passage, for in the

[15] Some passages in the coda were changed from triplets to thirty-second notes in the autograph, and must have been among Beethoven's last revisions in Op. 120.

Ex. 40

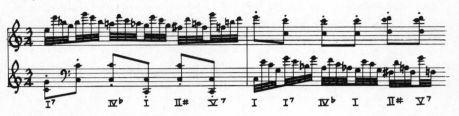

Ex. 41

finished work, the highest tones in each group of four sixteenths spell out, audibly, the thematic descending fourth G–D, in preparation for its final appearances on the tonic as C–G. In rounding off this gigantic cycle of variations, then, Beethoven saturates the texture of his music with the descending fourth—the motto, as it were, of both the Op. 111 Arietta and of the Diabelli Variations.

THE AUTOGRAPH (VARS. 29, 31)

At last we have arrived at the final stage in Beethoven's compositional process of the Variations: the autograph score. The autograph is on oblong eight-stave paper, Beethoven's normal format for piano autographs at this time.[16] Like the autograph of the Op. 111 Piano Sonata, the autograph of Op. 120 starts out as a very clean copy, with few revisions or changes, whereas toward the end of each work, evidence increases that Beethoven was still composing when he wrote out his ostensible final copies. In the piano sonata, this is particularly noticeable in the transition passage with trills to E flat, and near the final cadence in the Arietta. In Op. 120, most of the variations from No. 26 until the coda show extensive revisions in detail; and the two newly added slow variations from 1823, Nos. 29 and 31, underwent the actual process of composition in the autograph.

[16] The paper is unusual, however, in consisting of a type of Kiesling paper that does not appear in other autographs by Beethoven. I am indebted to Sieghard Brandenburg for this information.

One variation from the heart of the work, Var. 14, also shows obvious signs of being rewritten in the autograph, since it has been pasted over an earlier version. The problem here, however, seems not to have been one of musical substance but of clarity and accuracy in a manuscript that was to serve as the basis for the *Stichvorlage*. Beethoven had been careless in writing out the double dots used consistently throughout this variation; this can be seen from a portion of the earlier version crossed out by the composer but nevertheless partially legible. It seems to have disturbed Beethoven that this double-dotted rhythm might be incorrectly printed, and his concern was recorded not only in this rewritten score but by notes in the autograph, in the Engelmann Sketchbook, and in the *Abschrift* sent to Ries exhorting the careful transmission of this variation. The composer evidently did not give such careful attention to the following fifteenth variation, in which the apparent lack of a change of clef has stirred controversies about the correct text that are still unresolved today.[17]

Most of Beethoven's last-minute revisions in the variations toward the end of the set concern matters of detail: refinement of motivic working-out, changes in registral spacing, and even the rearrangement of parts on the staves in complicated passages in the Fugue. The first of the trilogy of minor variations, however, presents a more interesting case. This is one of several variations from the later period of composition that evoke an archaic atmosphere, and more specifically, the baroque idiom of J. S. Bach. The Adagio is through-composed without repetitions, and telescopes the opening tonic-dominant area from Diabelli's theme into two bars, so that only the barest outline of relation remains. In this space of freedom, Beethoven writes a kind of baroque lament, which could easily be imagined in a setting for a solo melody instrument and figured bass, as Ex. 42 shows.

Ex. 42

The passage revised by Beethoven in the autograph is the beginning of the second half, where there is a shift in register for the melody from treble to bass. In the first version of this passage, crossed out in the autograph, the melody remained in the treble; the texture, in typical baroque fashion, was stratified throughout. Beethoven's final solution, however, is more subtle, and

---

[17] See Chapter 8, below.

the exchange of parts at the beginning of the second half, as well as the richer harmonies that follow it, dispel the most obviously archaizing elements of the variation before they can take complete hold. Nevertheless, the exchange of parts in the autograph did not represent a new idea for Beethoven, but rather a reversion to an older one: in the draft of the passage, in Paris 57, the shift in register is already present.

The Largo variation, No. 31, another piece reminiscent of the baroque in general and J. S. Bach in particular, seems to have been the last variation in Op. 120 to be completed. In its second half, the music builds to an increase in tension enhanced by a chromatically rising bass and fantastically elaborate ornamentation of a fundamental linear progression. At this moment, as so often in the music of Beethoven's last period, these intricate constellations of sound coalesce into trills, and the melody, expressed wholly by pulsating trills, penetrates the highest register in attaining its thematic goal, outlining the tones of the tonic triad. It pauses on the dominant. Then, having scaled this height, this point of no return, Beethoven's autograph breaks off with a few brief, abortive sketches (Ex. 43). And here, poised on the brink of eternity, our study of the genesis of the Diabelli Variations draws to a close.

Ex. 43

PART II: THE COMPOSITIONAL STYLE

IV. The Late Compositional Style

THE music of Beethoven's last decade represents a departure in many respects from any music he had hitherto composed or, for that matter, from any that had previously existed. An inquiry into any one of these late masterpieces must confront unique features of this style, which represent less a rejection than a transformation of the aesthetic ideals of Beethoven's earlier works. By 1818 the composer's deafness was all but complete; the first of his conversation books dates from this period. As Beethoven's realization and acceptance of his impending deafness almost two decades before had contributed to the evolution in his art crowned by the 'Eroica' Symphony, so did the complete erosion of his hearing mark the beginning of the most profound episode in his creativity.[1]

What modifications in Beethoven's musical language account for the expansion of expressive possibilities in his late works? This question is bound up with a change in his treatment of musical form, and a restructuring of the underlying emotional progression that conditions it. Paradoxically, tendencies towards both dissociation and organic coherence vie for supremacy in many of these pieces, but in such a way that neither forecloses the other. Despite the complexity of this phenomenon, it is possible to isolate some of its basic features.

A striking aspect of Beethoven's late compositional style is his tendency to obscure formal landmarks within individual movements, such as cadences. In a sense, this tendency to avoid cadential articulation is itself the product of a concern with formal continuity applied to larger dimensions of the music. The denial or weakening of cadence, and the resulting lack of closure, provided Beethoven with a means of linking passages or movements even of drastically contrasting character. We have seen an obvious instance of this concern in Beethoven's draft for Vars. 19 and 21 of Op. 120, discussed above (see pp. 32–3). Another example is contained in the first movement of the Piano Sonata, Op. 109, where the contrasting thematic material in 'adagio' tempo is introduced at the moment of an interrupted cadence in the opening 'vivace' material, a cadence whose resolution is later supplied, in the same register, when the 'vivace' returns. In this instance, the interpolated material is much longer than the opening theme itself; it represents an internal expansion

---

[1] For a discussion of the main circumstances of Beethoven's life in this period, see Maynard Solomon, *Beethoven* (New York, 1977), especially pp. 217–30.

of the music at an interrupted cadence, permitting the bagatelle-like material of the 'vivace' to be extended to proportions suitable for the first movement of a sonata.

In two works, the Piano Sonata in A major, Op. 101, and the String Quartet in C sharp minor, Op. 131, Beethoven goes so far as to delay the first strong cadential downbeat in the tonic until the beginning of the last movement, creating a structural tension spanning the entire composition. The principle of delayed resolution is joined here by other aspects of the music to enhance the effect of cyclic unity: in the sonata, the introduction to the Finale recalls the texture of the opening slow movement, followed by an actual reminiscence of the first movement; in the quartet, where all of the movements are connected by subtle transitions in sonority, the Finale recalls the thematic substance and even the tonal structure of the opening Fugue.

Another distinctive aspect of Beethoven's late style is his control over the quality of sonority as a constitutive musical element, not in the Romantic sense of a sensuous play of sound, but as a conceptual background for the music itself. Reference to the particular quality or continuity of sound is used as a means of integration; in this respect, as in many others, Beethoven represents a synthesis of the old and the new, of the universality of the classical harmonic framework with the quest for particularity of expression characteristic of the nineteenth century. It is extraordinary that this sensitive control of sonority is most evident in the works of Beethoven's last decade, when he was completely deaf, and could hear only in his imagination.

A notable example of Beethoven's use of sonority as a structural and expressive principle is contained in the Credo of the *Missa Solemnis*. The striking opening gesture in the orchestra at the beginning of the Credo consists of an upward leap of an octave to a sustained E flat chord, with G in the highest voice, which subsequently resolves to the dominant sonority of B flat major. This E flat chord, in an identical spacing, recurs several times in the course of the movement in different contexts, first as a ritornello, but later as the very climax of the great 'Vitam Venturi' fugue, and finally as the setting for 'Amen' in the coda. The sound of the E flat chord is treated as a thematic element on the level of the whole movement.

From Beethoven's sketchbooks, it can be seen that the device of anticipating the climatic sonority from the fugue at the very beginning of the Credo was an idea conceived late in the process of composition, since it is absent from preliminary drafts of the work. In this instance, in his efforts to impose unity on a long and complex movement, Beethoven worked backwards from the end of the movement, the setting of 'Amen', and from its expressive centre, the climax of the fugue.[2] An analogous process of integration by means

---

[2] For a more detailed discussion of these relationships in the Mass, see William Kinderman, 'Beethoven's Symbol for the Deity in the Missa Solemnis and the Ninth Symphony', *19th-Century Music*, ix (1985), pp. 102–18.

of sonority can be observed in the Diabelli Variations, and here, once again, the relationship was devised after the creation of a preliminary draft. The crux of the relationship in the Variations is to the melodic outline and supporting context of Diabelli's waltz: in several of the variations written in 1823, these aspects of the theme are recalled in their original register. The sound of the waltz is recalled in a series of periodic references which serve both a recapitulatory and a parodistic function. These variations will be discussed below (see pp. 71–5).

In a sense, this reliance on sonority as a means of integration is evidence of Beethoven's fidelity to classical principles: a key sonority may be treated as a thematic musical element no less than an intervallic relationship or a motif. Beethoven's later works relentlessly exploit the procedures of thematic integration and unification forged by Haydn. In another sense, however, this music can seem decidedly unclassical when measured against Haydn and Mozart or Beethoven's own earlier works. The change in style is more than a matter of technical procedure; it represents a departure from the classical aesthetic framework, based as it was on balance, symmetry, and proportion.

Perhaps the most striking single aspect of Beethoven's late music is its tendency to replace symmetrical forms with a central climax by a musical progression leading to a final, culminating experience. The enclosure of symmetrical recapitulation, for example, is consistently challenged. In the opening sonata movements of the Quartets in A minor, Op. 132, and in B flat major, Op. 130, the harmonic stability of the thematic recapitulation is undercut; and in other examples Beethoven prepares the harmonic climax to take place after the moment of recapitulation, as in the 'Hammerklavier' Sonata.[3] In more 'traditional' examples, such as the first movement of the Ninth Symphony, Beethoven achieves the inverse effect—the moment of recapitulation is enhanced, the conditions of the opening transcended. This can also be observed in the decorated recapitulations of the slow variation movements in Opp. 111, 127, and 131, and most subtly in Op. 135.[4] A sense of return or of literal restatement, a procedure common in Beethoven's earlier music, is conspicuously avoided here.

Analogous departures shape the overall progression of movements in many of these pieces. The opening movements are frequently tentative, preparatory, even dissociated, and the centre of gravity is shifted to the finale. In Beethoven's earlier works, as in the classical style in general, the most weighty movement is almost invariably the first, whereas the finale is often relatively looseknit and unproblematical. In fact, a succession of movements following the general psychological scheme tension–resolution is characteristic not only

---

[3] See Rosen's analysis of Op. 106 in *The Classical Style*, pp. 409–14.
[4] These variation movements are discussed in William Kinderman, 'Tonality and Form in the Variation Movements of Beethoven's Late Quartets', *Beethoven-Symposion, Bonn 1984* (Bonn, forthcoming).

of Beethoven's historical age but that of many generations to follow: few composers of the nineteenth century explored the possibilities opened up by Beethoven's reversal of the conventional aesthetic sequence.

This new aesthetic—which amounted to a change in Beethoven's perception of the nature of music—arose during the years of personal introspection and fallow productivity that followed the completion of the Seventh and Eighth Symphonies and the Immortal Beloved crisis in 1812. The Song-cycle *An die ferne Geliebte* and the Piano Sonata Op. 101 are signposts on this new path; the 'Hammerklavier' Sonata, the *Missa Solemnis*, and the Diabelli Variations are among its major monuments.

It is within this context that the Op. 120 Variations need to be placed. The radical, titanic fugal Finale of the original version of the Quartet, Op. 130 with the *Grosse Fuge*; the end of the *Missa Solemnis*, with its ambiguous message underlined by threats to 'inner and outer peace'; the open-ended vision at the conclusion of the Arietta in the Piano Sonata, Op. 111—each of these is in a sense left 'unresolved', for the evolution of the work itself leaves no room for a return to the conditions of its initial stages. In a real sense, none of these works is bound as a formal whole. Each embodies an ongoing process, and ends not in satisfying resolution, but in pointed pregnancy of effect.

In the Ninth Symphony, the quotation and rejection of the themes of the previous movements demonstrate the purpose of the Finale as a transcendence of them. And even in the great C sharp minor Quartet, that pinnacle of 'absolute music', a sketchbook in Berlin records that Beethoven considered appending the theme in D flat later used in the Lento assai of Op. 135 as a coda to the Finale.[5] If this theme, identified by its author as 'süsser Rühegesang', had been placed at the end of the turbulent 'allegro' Finale, its effect would have been little short of programmatic, and akin to those drastic juxtapositions embodied in the original B flat Quartet and in the Mass.

In Beethoven's late works, he was willing to subordinate formal symmetry and aesthetic balance to immediacy of communication and ceaseless exploration into the hidden resources of musical art in quest of illumination. In this sense, the received nineteenth-century view of these works as chaotic and formless was quite literally correct. This same outlook judged Wagner's later works as destructive of form, and for essentially the same reasons. Both composers are indeed weak in 'form' regarded as an architectural framework imposed from without. The criticism of the later works of Beethoven and Wagner on these grounds is actually an indictment of their failure to obey the conventions of the day. But these pieces, among them the Diabelli Variations, are concerned with issues that loom larger than convention, and this accounts, at least in part, for their permanent human value.

[5] See Winter, 'Plans for the Structure of the String Quartet in C sharp Minor Op. 131', pp. 124-5. A more detailed discussion is contained in Winter, *Compositional Origins of Beethoven's Opus 131*, pp. 121-4; 167-74; 206-9.

In the Op. 120 Variations the idea of ascent through a progression of experiences is implicit in the basic 'idea', Beethoven's use of Diabelli's beer hall waltz as raw material and a point of departure. The theme itself is trivial. But as Tovey once pointed out, it is also 'rich in solid musical facts';[6] a reservoir of unrealized possibilities. It was left to Beethoven to discover these possibilities, and in so doing to open up entirely new vistas in the history of variation form. Beneath the surface, this seemingly implausible project stimulated the composer's deepest well-springs of imagination and inspiration.

An analytical study of the Diabelli Variations that seeks to elucidate decisive moments in its structure and organization cannot afford to ignore the preserved evidence from Beethoven's own compositional process. With this work—as, one suspects, with many others—it was only during the process of composition that Beethoven discovered creative possibilities which have no immediate precedent in his earlier music. The internal history of the composition reflects something of the same process experienced by the listener in its performance. It is therefore valuable for critical appraisal of the Variations to retrace the creative path traversed by Beethoven.

For two reasons, this approach yields special rewards in the case of Op. 120. On the one hand, the directional character of a large set of variations starting with the trivial but finally attaining the sublime dominates the overall form. As the piece moved toward completion, Beethoven strongly underscored its evolutionary character, and only then did he conceive of a suitable culmination for it. As we have seen, this kind of evolutionary scheme is entirely typical of Beethoven's third period. The thirty-three variations, however, represent an extreme case, which demanded an extremity of methods.

On the other hand, the divided chronology in composition of Op. 120 left a mark on this work whose significance may be gauged from a knowledge of Beethoven's compositional process. Prominent aspects of the work as we know it were first conceived by Beethoven in 1822–3, and superimposed upon an older plan. According to the evidence of the sketches and drafts, one third of the variations were composed years after the rest, and this information sheds a most interesting light upon the variations late in conception. They seem to represent a response to the formal problems of the entire set, and particularly to the discrepancy between the commonplace waltz and the formidable array of variations. In the end, this discrepancy was overcome; and in the process the Diabelli Variations became a masterpiece of subtlety and humour.

[6] Tovey, *Essays in Musical Analysis: Chamber Music* (London, 1944), p. 124.

V. The Importance of Parody

THE most interesting fact about the variations from 1822–3 is that most of them can be regarded as in some sense parodistic. The concept of parody is, however, a complex one, and there are several different kinds of parody at work in the Diabelli Variations. Parody of the theme in the set of variations, in the sense of mockery, was of course well known to Beethoven long before he embarked on the composition of Op. 120. One example from among many, is Beethoven's burlesque of the theme in the thirteenth variation of the 'Eroica' set, Op. 35, from 1802, and in this case the humour is increased by the fact that the theme stems from the composer himself. In the Diabelli set on the other hand, thematic parody is used in an unprecedented way, to shape the overall form of the work.

The matter of parody in Op. 120 has been treated by Lars Ulrich Abraham in a provocative article, 'Trivialität und Persiflage in Beethovens Diabelli-Variationen'.[1] Abraham points out the banality of Diabelli's theme, and its fitness for caricature. He also isolates elements of 'persiflage' in Beethoven's opening march variation, particularly the static but pompous bass octaves in the opening phrase (quoted in Ex. 47 below). His identification of 'persiflage' in the other variations is frequently arbitrary, however. He does not require that 'persiflage' in a variation should bear an immediately audible kinship to the theme; as a result, many of Beethoven's characteristic departures from Diabelli's waltz are wrongly accounted as travesty of the theme. For Abraham, the opening of Var. 10 is a 'crass caricature' of Diabelli,[2] but those aspects he counts as evidence of travesty—the tremolo in the right hand and descending octave scale in the left—have no direct relation to the waltz. Similarly, the mysterious pause on a diminished-seventh chord in the second half of Var. 3, and the modulation to the mediant at the end of the first half of Var. 5 are regarded as 'persiflage'. Actually, they are merely different from the theme, and in no sense a travesty of it. Examples could be multiplied—Abraham finds 'persiflage' in the opening bars of at least half the variations. Because of its methodological rigidity, Abraham's article is the *reductio ad absurdum* of a basically sound idea, and though it has brought attention to this important and neglected aspect of the piece, it does not begin to do justice to it.

A more promising approach is to first reassess the concept of parody in general. In the classical sense of the word *para odos*, as in *Parodiemesse*, it

[1] *Neue Wege der musikalischen Analyse* (Berlin, 1967), pp. 7–17. [2] Abraham, p. 10.

implies re-use, and not travesty.[3] We should not associate parody inevitably with humour; Beethoven's use of parody embraces a gamut of effects, and each case needs to be judged on its own merits. What is a fundamental aspect of parody, however, is the allusion that points beyond itself; with or without irony, such an evocation enjoys a complex existence between two modes of being—literal, and referential. This referential aspect of parody lends a concrete sense of the world background to art, and it even admits the entrance of a moral factor, as in homage, or caricature.

It is perhaps on account of these qualities that the ageing Beethoven was drawn so frequently to parody. Critics who have come to grips with these pieces, such as Riezler, and Kerman, have been impressed by their profound subjective realism and, if we follow Adorno, their subjective contingency. Some of the most characteristic strokes in these works depend vitally on effects that can only be called parodistic.

A familiar, and to many listeners, still startling example of Beethoven's use of parody is the B flat 6/8 variation in the Finale of the Ninth Symphony. The 'Turkish' orchestration trivializes the hymn-like theme, and off-beat accents confirm their humorous effect at the hasty cadences. The unforgettable vividness of this scherzo section owes much to the Shakespearean juxtaposition of a comic military march with the solemnity of the grand pause on the words 'und der Cherub steht vor Gott', immediately preceding it (the juxtaposition of key contributes substantially to this, too). Furthermore, the parody contributes a dimension of authenticity, of factuality, to Beethoven's interpretation of the text. The words spoken by the tenor are cheerful and naïve ('Froh, froh', etc.), but the music, though cheerful, is not exactly conceived in naïvety, since it is a transformation, and a distortion, of the principal theme of the movement. The joyfulness of this variation is not quite real.

In the Diabelli Variations, we can distinguish at least two kinds of travesty, and at least two other kinds of parody. Not all of these involve parody of Diabelli. The comic variation on Mozart's 'Notte e giorno faticar' in Var. 22 is a parody of Mozart (Beethoven's ambivalent feelings about *Don Giovanni* are well known). Another evocation that points beyond Diabelli's theme is Var. 23, which imitates the idiom of an étude in the style of J. B. Cramer. In several of the last variations, on the other hand, we confront an evocation of previous historical styles, such as the reference to Bach's Goldberg Variations in the last of the slow minor variations, or to Mozart in the Minuet finale. Again, these are not pointed references to the theme itself, and they can scarcely be regarded as 'persiflage' of the original waltz.

[3] For a discussion of the concept of parody—or *imitatio*—in the sixteenth century, see Lewis Lockwood, 'On "Parody" as Term and Concept in 16th-Century Music', *Aspects of Medieval and Renaissance Music: A Birthday Offering to Gustav Reese*, ed. Jan LaRue (New York, 1966), pp. 560–75.

In other variations, however, there is a direct travesty to the theme. The first four bars of Var. 21, for example, form a grotesque exaggeration of the primitive chord repetitions in the waltz and its conventional turn at the head of the melody. The chords repeat each harmony sixteen times, the turns multiply themselves down three octaves. The juxtaposition of this passage with the following Meno allegro in 3/4 is one of those instances in Beethoven's late music in which the notes speak with rhetorical significance (see Ex. 44). It is as if Beethoven meant to say, after the *Schreckensfanfare* of the first four bars, 'nicht diese Töne'.[4]

Ex. 44

Another parody variation, Var. 13, is imbued with humorous intention, as Charles Rosen has pointed out.[5] In it, the harmonically static bars of Diabelli's opening theme are suppressed altogether, obliterated into the silence behind rhythmically charged chords (Ex. 45). In this variation, the sheer strength of Beethoven's rhythmic conception makes a mockery of Diabelli's theme, and the inconsequential complacency of its opening bars. The humour of the variation consists in its expressive use of silence: our expectations are alternatively strained by the menacing gesture of the chords, and then dissipated into nothing.[6] This variation, like Var. 21, is a travesty of the inadequacy of the theme, and a provisional gesture towards a transcendence of it.

Ex. 45

[4] The idea of the *Schreckensfanfare* is of course not confined to Beethoven's Ninth Symphony. See Harry Goldschmidt, *Die Erscheinung Beethoven* (Leipzig, 1974), p. 109.

[5] *The Classical Style*, p. 95.

[6] The humour of expressive silences exploited in this variation is foreshadowed by the bass theme that opens the 'Eroica' Variations, Op. 35.

In Beethoven's late work on the Variations he introduced another kind of travesty distinct from the examples of Vars. 13 and 21. Here, Beethoven harps on the actual substance of the waltz itself—specifically those features of it which are particularly trite—and reproduces them in exaggerated form so that they become insufferably so in the parody. It is this form of parody that is most important for the overall progression of the Variations, because Beethoven's criterion for criticism is precisely the melodic outline of Diabelli's theme. Most of Beethoven's other variations thoroughly transform the surface of Diabelli's theme, and though motivic materials from the waltz are exploited exhaustively, its affective model is left far behind. In these late parody variations, however, the melodic outline and supporting context from the waltz are restored—recapitulated, in a sense—and they stand out because of Beethoven's consistent suppression of these features in the other variations. Only in the added variations, furthermore, does the melodic outline of the waltz reappear in its original register, which strengthens the reference to the theme.[7] Diabelli returns, as it were—the material is not Beethoven's—but he returns in a different *Stimmung*, a kind of Lisztian transformation.

This last form of parody is the most subtle, since it embodies Beethoven's basic cultural judgement of the waltz. It has frequently been overlooked (even by someone on the look-out for 'persiflage', such as Abraham). But with the evidence from Beethoven's early compositional plan before us, it is easy to discern the motivation behind his insertion of several of these travesty variations, and that, in turn, further clarifies the nature of the variations themselves.

When Beethoven returned to composition of the Variations in 1822-3, he confronted a unique formal dilemma. Beethoven normally strove to endow the opening of any major work with a pregnant tension and significance; the Op. 120 Variations are the great exception, an outstanding example of a major work with origins in the commonplace. But these variations are not confined to the possibilities of Diabelli's theme *per se*. The nature of the theme in no way anticipates the scope and immensity of the Variations. How then was Beethoven to establish a relationship between the theme and variations such that the waltz was not rendered superfluous, as a mere prologue to the whole? This implicit contradiction may have had something to do with Beethoven's uncharacteristic decision to lay this work aside for several years. But in any case, the apparent absurdity of building a monumental edifice upon such slight foundations had, by 1823, supplied an unexpected stimulus to Beethoven's own imagination.

By parodying the theme directly, with its melodic contours intact, Beethoven made the waltz itself into an indispensable foundation for the

---

[7] This effect of a return to the original sonority of the waltz would have been even more evident heard on pianos of the early nineteenth century, with their characteristically uneven sound in different registers, than on the modern piano.

overall musical progression. In fact, in the work we know, all of the supporting pillars of the overall form depend upon the recapitulation of the melodic
shape of Diabelli's theme. In this way, the listener's first impression of the
theme is utilized in a way not unlike Beethoven's procedure in other variation
sets, such as the C minor Variations, Wo 80, in which a series of recapitulatory references to the theme embrace the work as a whole. In the Diabelli
Variations, moreover, the last of these recapitulatory references presented an
ideal point of departure for an evolutionary progression leading to a final,
culminating experience. The project was, therefore, in a peculiar way, tailor-
made to fit the revolutionary aesthetic of Beethoven's third period.

A conspicuous characteristic of the waltz recalled in these added variations
from 1823 is the repeated tonic chord with highest tone G that opens the
dance (see Ex. 46). This G, repeated ten times in the first four bars, continues as
the highest note of the dominant chords in the next four-bar phrase. The
static harmonic scheme of the waltz is underscored by these repeated chords,
with their persistent emphasis on G. It is not surprising that Beethoven should
depart from this static aspect of the waltz in most of his variations. What is
remarkable is that in the variations added later, Beethoven adopts and
exaggerates precisely these features of the waltz.

Ex. 46

We are now in a position to judge the reason for Beethoven's insertion of a
vigorous, majestic variation Alla marcia maestoso immediately after Diabelli's
waltz. The refined third variation, originally planned as the first, did nothing
to smooth over the discrepancy between theme and variations, since it is
already such a thorough transformation of the theme. But in his singular
solution of adding the march variation, Beethoven achieved a sense of gesture,
of grand anticipation, though one tinged with irony, since the melodic
contours of Diabelli's theme are so clearly preserved in the variation (see
Ex. 47). This pointed reference to the waltz is unmistakable. Beethoven would

Ex. 47

not otherwise have allowed himself nine consecutive repetitions of the tonic
triad in root position in the right hand, while the bass motion solemnly spelled
out the descending fourth of the waltz, creating accented harmonic clashes
with the treble. The grand gesture is simultaneously a parody of the theme.

It is only after this opening march variation that the melodic outlines of
Diabelli's theme—with its falling fourth and fifth and persistent emphasis on
the dominant note G—are avoided. In some variations, such as the third and
the eighth, the melodic line is reshaped as a descent from the third, E, of the
tonic triad. In others, manifold changes in texture, harmony, and rhythm
leave only a tenuous link between the melody and its successive transformations. It is therefore a significant event when Beethoven finally
recapitulates the melodic contour of the theme in Var. 15, the Presto
scherzando, and then again in the paired variations that follow it. Var. 15,
unlike the paired variations, also brings a return of the melodic outline of the
waltz in its original register. Vars. 16 and 17 were present in the PLM Draft, as
we have seen; but Var. 15, like Var. 1, was an afterthought, added to the piece
as it was nearing completion.

If the opening march variation is a mock-heroic gesture bearing the seeds
of irony, this Presto scherzando (Ex. 48) is an even more obvious caricature of

Ex. 48

the theme itself. Its character as a miniature juxtaposed with two of the most
massive variations (No. 14 and the pair 16-17) reinforces its parodistic
quality, as does its unusually static harmonic plan—the first half actually
closes on the tonic! Furthermore, its harmonic rhythm is rather peculiar in its
alternation of the tonic triad with an augmented triad on the dominant. In its
linear-harmonic structure, it mimics the simple C(I)-D(V)-E(I)-D(V)-C(I)

progression from Diabelli's theme,[8] and this is underscored by a capricious increase in spacing in the second half.

This reference to the theme is broadened into a more general allusion in the pair of march variations immediately after Var. 15. The sequence of Vars. 15–17 is counterpoised to the sequence of the theme and Var. 1, which is also a march (though, to be sure, a march with a rather different, more stilted character). In a curious, elusive way, this long-range correspondence draws Diabelli's theme more closely into the fabric of the work.

The waltz finds its final reincarnation in Var. 25, where it appears in the guise of a German dance, with the rhythm of Diabelli's bass shifted to the treble. Beethoven's tongue-in-cheek attitude is perhaps even more obvious here than in Var. 15. Monotony of rhythm, dissonant clashes between treble and bass, and aimlessness in the voice-leading confirm Beethoven's humorous intention. At the end of the first variation half, the composer goes so far as to omit a bar before the cadence, causing the music to stumble prematurely back to the beginning (Ex. 49).

Ex. 49

This lumbering caricature of Diabelli's theme is actually the first of an unbroken succession of variations (Nos. 25–33) leading to the coda and culmination of the work. In fact a thread of continuity, tracing the path from banality to sublimity—from the world of Diabelli's ditty to the world of the Arietta from Op. 111—sounds through all of these last nine variations. By extraordinary means, as we shall see, Beethoven first obliterated his distorted image of the theme, and then gradually reconstituted its essence in a series of variations that culminates in the last of the slow minor variations, the penultimate Fugue, and the concluding Minuet and coda.

Beethoven's overall formal progression is shown in Fig. 5, where the new variations are indicated by a square bracket. In this unique structure Diabelli's waltz is treated first ironically as a march that is half-stilted, half-impressive, and then, at crucial points in the form, twice recapitulated in amusing caricature variations. At the conclusion of the work, in the Fugue and last variation, reference to the melodic head of Diabelli's theme once again becomes explicit—indeed, it is hammered into the ground. But any further sense of the

---

[8] See the analysis of Diabelli's waltz, pp. 78–80 below.

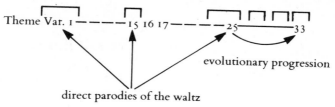

evolutionary progression

direct parodies of the waltz

FIG. 5. Overall formal progression of Op. 120.

original context of the waltz is lacking. By means of the three parody variations, 1, 15, and 25, Beethoven established a series of periodic references to the waltz that draw it more closely into the inner workings of the set, and the last of these gives rise to a progression that transcends the theme once and for all. This is the central idea of the Diabelli Variations.

VI. Beethoven's Treatment of the Theme

In his essay on Op. 120,[1] Donald Francis Tovey devoted considerable care to the 'solid musical facts' of Diabelli's theme, and the means of their appropriation by Beethoven. Every one of Diabelli's motives is exploited to the utmost in Op. 120, and consequently an intimate relation exists between the variations and theme despite Beethoven's great freedom of treatment. Beethoven's debt to the waltz is not confined to these motives, but they form an indispensable starting-point for analysis.

The basic motives utilized by Beethoven and cited by Tovey comprise (a) the opening turn; (b) the descending fourth and fifth from the first phrases of the melody; (c) the related ascending fourths from the bass line; (d) the sequences that initiate modulation away from and back to the tonic. These are shown in Ex. 50.

Ex. 50

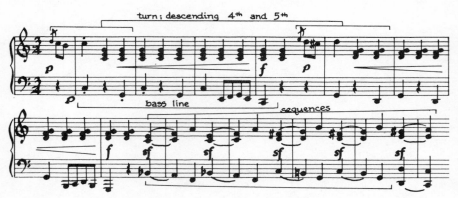

One or more of these structural elements from the theme is employed in each of the variations, where a process of concentration and discrimination is evident. In Vars. 9, 11, and 12, the turn figure, a mere accessory in the waltz, becomes the basis for the musical texture. On the other hand, the original form of the 'cobbler's patch' sequences, which aroused Beethoven's scorn, is maintained in only one variation, No. 19. In two variations, Nos. 3 and 11,

---

[1] *Essays in Musical Analysis: Chamber Music* (London, 1944), pp. 124-34.

Beethoven reproduces (and exaggerates) the distinctive syncopations from the waltz by the use of notes tied over the bar-line. Examples could be multiplied; we shall dwell here only on the most central and cogent relationships.

Beethoven's use of Diabelli's bass line is more often than not confined to its basically iambic rhythm:

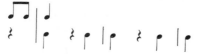

In the sequence of Vars. 4–6, this pattern is emphasized in a way which draws increasing emphasis to the quarter-note upbeat, and shows how a rhythmic element from the theme is developed in a short series of successive variations.

Towards the end of the set various thematic elements are synthesized and combined in astonishing ways. Var. 25 adapts the melody of the waltz with the rhythm of Diabelli's bass line, and draws on the turn figure as its own bass (Ex. 51). The three subjects of the triple Fugue relate to the three different

Ex. 51

fundamental aspects of the waltz: the melody, with its falling fourth and repeated emphasis on the dominant; the sequences, which in the Fugue descend instead of ascend; and the turn, which comprises much of the substance of the faster motion of the last subject. These are shown in Ex. 52. This Fugue is a *tour de force* in its synthesis of basic thematic elements which are combined with contrapuntal rigour and dramatic power.

Most important of all motivic relations between the variations and theme are the descending fourth and fifth, which in the second half of the waltz are inverted to an ascending fifth and sixth. So fundamental are these intervals

Ex. 52

that in Var. 20, the mysterious quiet Andante in which practically all textural and rhythmic ties to the waltz are broken, their presence, repeated in canon, ensures an audible relationship to the theme. In the parody Vars. 1 and 15, these intervals are reproduced almost verbatim from the waltz, with the exception of the ascending sixth G–E in the second half. The sixth, however, assumes a crucial role at the end of Beethoven's coda (see Ex. 53). In the closing bars, Beethoven bids farewell to the waltz, and to the entire cycle of variations, by a final reminiscence of the descending fourth C–G, and then the ascending sixth G–E, which is embodied in the last two chords of the work.

Ex. 53

We are now in a position to go beyond Tovey's 'solid musical facts' to examine Beethoven's interpretation of the total shape of Diabelli's waltz. This last structural tie to Diabelli—the descending fourth and fifth in the first half balanced by an ascending fifth and sixth in the second—derives force from its role as part of the overall linear progression of Diabelli's waltz, a matter passed over in silence by Tovey. This is, however, of central importance. In order to perceive the basis for Beethoven's most striking departures from Diabelli, and particularly his harmonic innovations, we shall need to evaluate, as he did, the linear and harmonic parameters of the waltz.

Diabelli's theme has been disparaged, and not without reason; but its primitive virtues should not be overlooked. Its rustic vitality and clear-cut motives lend themselves well to variation and, for that matter, to parody. Another fruitful aspect of the theme is the interesting ambiguity in its linear structure. Perhaps its most obvious characteristic is the reiteration of chords with highest note G that dominates the opening of the dance. This G, repeated ten times in the first four measures, continues as highest tone of the dominant chords in the next phrase, and even the 'cobbler's patch' sequences that follow lead to the dominant note G at the cadence of the first half. In the second half, however, this bias toward the dominant note largely disappears. The repeated chords, now inverted, reach instead to the third of the tonic, E, and the role of the fifth in the closing bars is undermined by an upward shift in register. The fifth, which is a kind of static focal point in the voice-leading of the first half, is relatively unimportant in the second.

At the same time, the third, E, plays a somewhat more consistent role. The turn at the head of the opening tonic and dominant phrases of the theme passes upward from C to D. The series of sequences follow, leading to the dominant and the close of the first half of the waltz. But since this sequential passage is confined to the middle register, and rises no higher than D, the return of the four-bar phrases in the second half, raising the line from D(V)–E(I^{b7}), sounds like a continuation of the fundamental line C(I)–D(V) at the beginning of the theme. A returning descent from E to C subsequently occurs in the last three bars immediately following a reiteration of the pattern of ascent from tonic to mediant, although it, too, is rather weakened by the upward shift in register. Thus the underlying linear structure for Diabelli's theme is the straightforward progression C(I)–D(V)–E(I^{b7})–D(V)–C(I), although this in no way minimizes the persistent dominant emphasis of the repeated chords in its first half (see Ex. 54).

In the Variations, Beethoven frequently adopts a linear progression based on the third of the tonic triad, as we shall see when we treat them in detail. Most often, however, he incorporates a striking harmonic change into the thematic structure of the second half in bar 21, where Diabelli arrives at the peak and goal of his progression. In the waltz, this is a C major triad that becomes a seventh chord with the addition of B flat in the bass two bars later, and it is then treated as V of IV, resolving to an F major triad at the beginning of the sequences immediately following. Hardly any of Beethoven's variations reproduce Diabelli's harmonies at this point, although the subdominant goal remains unchanged in all but a few of them. Beethoven usually substitutes a diminished–seventh chord E–G–B^b–D^b for the I^{b7}, and in a few instances draws upon a full minor-ninth chord as V of IV. Placement of either of these dissonant sonorities at this position in the form considerably increases the musical tension, and some of the most dramatic passages in the variations depend upon the ambiguity of this diminished seventh and the C–D flat semitone conflict embodied in the minor–ninth chord.

This moment, in fact, comprises the harmonic climax in numerous variations. In Var. 5, for example, the I^{b9} chord releases explosive dissonance that helps carry the music into the key of the Neapolitan, D flat (see Ex. 55).

Ex. 54

Ex. 55

Var. 9 (in the minor) contains a sustained modulation to D flat in its second half, and in it Beethoven exploits the intrinsic ambiguity of the diminished-seventh chord cited above, as he feigns possible resolutions to C, and then again to D, by the enharmonic reinterpretation of D flat as C sharp (Ex. 56). In Var. 12 this C–D flat relation is expressed by the perpetual motion of a turn in the bass, producing a dark and dissonant rumble beneath syncopated chords in the highest register (Ex. 57). The climax of Var. 14 occurs as the root tone C of a I^{b7} chord is suddenly raised to C sharp, while the effect is heightened by dynamics and spacing (Ex. 58). A haunting phrase in Var. 30, one that Beethoven chose to repeat even after he excised repetitions from the rest of the variation, is based again on the same sonority (Ex. 59).

Ex. 56

Ex. 57

Ex. 58

Ex. 59

Perhaps one of the best examples of Beethoven's harmonic innovation, and its relation to linear structure, is presented by what was originally his first variation: Var. 3. This is one of those variations in which Beethoven undermined the stability of the opening tonic sonority of the theme by changing its position. The melodic line, beginning on the third, E, traces the outline of a triad in second inversion, and the supporting bass, after touching C on the first beat of the first bar ascends immediately to the dominant note G (see Ex. 60). Subsequently, the second four-bar phrase sinks easily into the dominant, with

Ex. 60

a drop of the fundamental line from E to D. But when the upper line descends again, it is only a semitone, to D flat, and this chromatic descent is supported by the diminished-seventh chord important in so many variations.

A return to this crucial sonority is made in the second half of the variation. In the first four bars of this half, Beethoven intensifies the texture from the opening of the variation by increasing the number of voices to three, and by exploiting the high upper register of the piano. The dominant-seventh chord with which this phrase ends demands resolution to the tonic, and is in fact resolved in the same register, but only later, in the closing bar of the variation. For suddenly this progression is broken off, and in the dark lower register the bass reiterates a prominent rhythmic motive as an ostinato, accompanied by the same diminished chord that had occurred in the first half of the variation. This passage is the first of many musical events in Op. 120 in which a mysterious, uncanny side of Beethoven's art comes to the surface. The effect is heightened by the interruption, at this point, of the expected arrival of the tonic sonority. These bars based on the diminished-seventh chord sound like a kind of internal expansion of the musical progression at an interrupted cadence, whose resolution is finally supplied in the last bar.

The single most telling departure from the thematic model undertaken by Beethoven, and the one most consistently maintained by him throughout the set, is this substitution of a diminished-seventh chord for the I^{b7} chord under E in the second half of Diabelli's theme. For this reason, the restoration of the ascending sixth G–E from the theme in Beethoven's Minuet finale and coda has a resolving effect. In the final chord of the work, the dissonance of the diminished-seventh is purged at last, and the tonic triad reigns as master. This close is harmonically satisfying because it stands in place of the dissonance which represented, throughout the Variations, a peak of harmonic tension.

Beethoven's other departures from the waltz need to be considered within the context of the individual variations and their contribution to the overall progression of the work. Relationship with the theme is never entirely lost in any of them, although it is often considerably strained, and in the closing variations, permanently altered. Most fundamental of all will be the melodic hallmarks of the fourth, fifth, and sixth from the waltz, the same intervals which found their way into that related contemporary variation work by Beethoven—the Arietta from his last Piano Sonata in C minor, Op. 111, of 1822. In Op. 120, the power of these fundamental relationships, joined by the extra-musical presence of humorous parody of the theme, impart unity to one of Beethoven's most dissociated works. We shall try to trace the means by which this is achieved by more detailed scrutiny of the thirty-three variations.

VII. The Opening Variations

THE pompous march Alla marcia maestoso that opens the set is a finely crafted piece despite its intentional parody. The octaves for the left hand in the first two phrases are a composing-out of the intervals of a fourth and fifth from the head of Diabelli's waltz. Thus the first phrases of this variation echo the theme in its descending fourth and fifth while at the same time easing the transition from Diabelli's theme into the variations by their static harmony. In fact, our first indication of Beethoven's sensitivity to the relations between variations is to be sought in the first four bars of the first two variations, and in their relationship to the theme. In both these variations, sustained tonic harmony in the chords on strong beats carries over from the waltz the effect of a static block of sound. And like the theme, but unlike most of the variations to follow, these pieces begin with the unambiguous statement of the full tonic triad in root position.

It is interesting to observe how Var. 1 utilizes and emphasizes the linear voice-leading pattern in the theme, namely the ascent and descent from the third, E, which we have discussed above. At the outset the upward movement from C(I) to D(V) is brought out by sustained, accented chords, and these accents return to reinforce a repetition of this ascent in the sequential passage that follows (bars 9-12). In the second half, the line, starting on D, climbs through an entire octave to high D, also punctuated by accents, before the return to the tonic from the third degree. As a result, the linear progression from Diabelli's theme here receives more precise definition, and even Beethoven's dynamic accents serve to underscore it.

Another striking aspect of this opening variation is its rhythmic vitality. This derives in large measure from the rhythmic ambiguity of the second chord in each bar, which sounds like an aftershock from the chords preceding, but also like an upbeat preparation for the next downbeat. This kind of rhythmic overlapping supplies an urgency of motion to a variation that would otherwise suffer from rhythmic monotony due to constant repetition of the same pattern throughout. Beethoven's echo effects play on this rhythmic ambiguity, and in the second half provide a faint suggestion of a slackening in the rhythmic drive with the addition in the echoed phrases of an appoggiatura and its resolution, as Ex. 61 shows. This character piece, however, drives resolutely to its conclusion, with pomp and fanfare.

Ex. 61

We know from the sketches that the second variation was one of the last composed by Beethoven, and its structural role is ostensibly to supply a transition from the heroic irony of the march to the subtle world of Vars. 3, 4 and 5. In keeping with his usual practice in variation sets, Beethoven prefers a gradually measured departure from the musical parameters of the theme, and in this delicate, restrained variation he returns to the original 3/4 metre, which is then maintained in the next six pieces (and in ten of the next eleven). Harmonically, this variation strongly anticipates Var. 3, especially in its first half, where even the voice-leading and register correspond. Perhaps this motivated Beethoven's decision to omit the repetition from its first half. Syncopated throughout, its greatest rhythmic complication occurs at the sequential passage in the second half (Ex. 62). The additional syncopation introduced here between the hands was a last-minute adjustment by the composer in the autograph, and it brings attention to the harmonic progression in these bars, with a shift to the mediant, E. In fact, linear emphasis on E can be noted throughout the second half of the variation, and the variation ends poised melodically on the third of the triad. This is the first of many instances in Op. 120 where the end of one variation subtly anticipates the beginning of the next.

Ex. 62

In this case, the emphasis on E in the second variation prepares the very opening of Var. 3, in which the opening phrase of the theme is reshaped as a descent from the third. In general, the ageing Beethoven paid particular attention to the sonorous transition between movements of his works, and this applies just as well to the Diabelli Variations as to the late quartets. The existence of such relationships between the variations also carries implications for their performance: long and arbitrary pauses between the variations should be avoided, lest these obscure the sensitive progression (or drastic opposition!) prepared in the notes themselves.

Even in Beethoven's very earliest sketches, Vars. 3 and 4 are juxtaposed, and they are indeed interrelated. Perhaps the most important aspects of this relationship are the increased rhythmic animation and expanded contrapuntal texture of Var. 4. The increase in rhythmic verve is reflected by Beethoven's tempo indication, 'un poco più vivace', implying a slight accelerando from the 'poco allegro' of the previous two variations. In contrast to the prevailing quarter-note motion of the previous two variations, we now encounter the pattern 𝄽 𝄽 a pulse punctuating the downbeats throughout, with the exception only of the pre-cadential hemiola before the cadence to the first part. The contrapuntal texture from Var. 3, moreover, is expanded from three to as many as five imitative entries spanning the whole compass of the keyboard. For the first time virtuosity begins to play a role in the drive toward the cadence to the second part, and here, in order to generate momentum that will carry into the next variation, Beethoven omits the hemiola.

Most extraordinary about Var. 4 is the way in which it suspends the lower-level phrase divisions of the theme. Each half of the variation is through-composed as one organism, and through internal development and insistent rhythm justifies the long crescendo to the end of each part. How does Beethoven achieve such cohesion? In the first half he arrives at the dominant one bar early by treating the final G of the last imitative entry as the true bass of the harmony. This dissolves the rigid selectional divisions of the thematic model while realizing the natural harmonic implications of his material. Furthermore, the next sectional break in the theme at the beginning of the ascending sequences is smoothed over in the variation by a deceptive cadence to the submediant, and the anticipation of the sequential melodic material one bar before. But most crucial to the urgent intensity of this passage is its ascending bass, advancing from G to A, and eventually to the dominant of the dominant, D. In contrast to the preceding variation, where the melodic treble line is predominant, here the bass seems to supply the principal linear impetus, and its pattern of ascent is echoed by the other parts. This basic harmonic-linear structure generates energy, and by means quite different from those used in its companion Var. 3, as can be seen if we abstract just the beginning of each progression:

The measured repose and then increasing dynamism of these variations leads to the brilliant impetuosity of Var. 5. The polyphonic texture of this variation is distinguished by voice entries with an upbeat of two repeated notes, representing in this faster tempo another stage in the progressive compression of the upbeat (it will be reduced to a trill in the next piece to come). The first phrase ends, strikingly, not on the tonic or dominant but on a dissonant diminished-seventh chord supporting C sharp; hence it is the function of the second phrase to resolve the first (see Ex. 63). This produces an intimate interrelationship between the phrases, especially since the end of the first and head of the second combine to spell out, audibly, the turn figure from Diabelli's waltz in augmentation.

Ex. 63

In this piece, for the first time since the march parody, Beethoven returns to the tonic harmony at the end of the second phrase. This conservatism is outweighted, however, by a modulation to E minor at the end of the first half. In fact, the prominence of the third, E, in the melodic voice-leading of the previous variation (due in part to the consequence of the rising bass motion to A) seems to prepare, subtly, for this modulation. The final cadence of that piece skips down abruptly a fifth; the note E seems to be implied but omitted. Four bars from the end of the first half of the fifth variation, the E is sounded in the same register, at the initiation of the modulation to the mediant. This is one evidence of the relationship between these variations.[1]

Another is the increasing galvanization of the rhythm. The pointed rhythmic upbeat of two eighth notes repeated in different voices, builds a cumulative tension that renders the downbeat unstable. In the second half, on the other hand, an enforced pianissimo and an eightfold upbeat repetition produce a hushed expectancy shattered by accentuated octave chords which carry over the rhythmic stress to the second beat of the bar. Beethoven builds

---

[1] Another, more obvious linear bond between successive variations spans Vars. 5 and 6. In the second half of Var. 5, following the tonicization of E, the note F is left unresolved at the final cadence. In bar 5 of Var. 6, the F is re-established emphatically, and carried forth in the voice-leading of that variation.

an intimate relation between these antecedent and consequent eight-bar phrases not on similarity, not even on continuity, but upon the realization, in an extreme form, of expectations of development implicit in the pregnant rhythms of the opening. The accents and dissonant clashes in the consequent phrase in the second half suddenly accelerate the rhythmic pulse threefold, which generates great excitement, and provides forceful release for the accumulated tension. Var. 5 is founded on a kind of dramatic dialectic, predominently rhythmic in nature.

Like the foregoing variations, this piece utilizes the tonic six-four chord as a point of departure, and submits it to another interpretation:

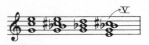

The modulation to E minor, however, is guided most strongly by the stepwise ascent of the bass from the dominant pedal of the first eight bars to A (following Var. 4) and then to B, dominant of the mediant.

This variation, then, is by no means devoid of relationship with the preceding pieces. In fact, it has more in common with them than with the variations immediately following.[2] From Vars. 2–5, we have observed a gradual intensification in dramatic expression based on subtle musical relationships. By contrast, the next two variations represent a simplification in substance, even as they introduce an expansion in sonorous exploitation of the instrument. The note of virtuosity present in the second part of Var. 5 is now carried forth in a pair of virtuosic variations, Nos. 6 and 7.

The sound of the first of these is spare and harsh, relieved only by a two-bar dolce codetta at the end of each half. This piece comes from the world of the fugal Finale of Op. 106 and the fugal Allegro from Op. 111—with the former it shares thematic use of the trill at the head of the theme, with the latter its sinuous sequential passage-work based on turn figures outlining diminished and minor harmonies. In the opening canonic phrases (see Ex. 64), a trill on the leading note grates against C major arpeggios in both voices, and in all registers.

It is revealing that Beethoven affixed the word 'serioso' to the tempo indication for this variation. The stern brilliance of its canonic texture, endowed with fierce energy but devoid of pathos, makes it hard for the listener. One of the most extreme sentiments in the palette of affects of Beethoven's late music is the roughly-hewn counterpoint infused with rhythmic force and strain. Here, however, the texture gradually relents, yield-

---

[2] This provides even more evidence of the inadequacy of symmetrical groupings based on four variations, such as was proposed by Geiringer ('The Structure of Beethoven's Diabelli Variations', *Musical Quarterly*, l (1964), pp. 496–503). It makes no musical sense to place a structural break after the fourth variation.

Ex. 64

Allegro, ma non troppo e serioso

ing finally to the warmth and consolation of full-voiced harmonic sounds in the codetta.

The last strains of Var. 6 lead directly, and in the same register, into Var. 7, in which the rhythmic impact of robust octaves in the bass gives rise to virtuosic passage-work in the treble. The main idea of this variation is rhythmic, and is expressed by the rhythmic relations between the two hands:

As hammer-blows yield reverberations, so strong single downbeats give rise to a continuous flow of pulsations. This variation exploits the tension between the defining downbeat, by its very nature singular, and its rhythmic antipode in a plurality of impulses. With physical immediacy, the last of the three accented octaves in the bass motivates a whirlwind of triplets stressing every beat (Ex. 65). In this passage the descending pitch of each triplet reflects the rhythmic decay of these pulsations from the octave downbeat that gave them their own impetus. Through these means Beethoven is able to express the diffusion of rhythmic energy by manipulataion of the musical parameter of pitch. This imparts a sublime grandeur to the variation.

Ex. 65

Un poco più allegro

In the sequences that follow these bars Beethoven alters the repetitions so that the first notes of each statement of the motif trace a chromatic ascent, and the harmonies are changed accordingly (Ex. 66). Here too, the sense of a controlling order deeper than the melodic surface is much in evidence. The mechanical phrase repetitions from the waltz are abolished. Even the integrity of the motive is subtly distorted at the call of more fundamental relationships.[3]

Ex. 66

The excited, agitated sentiment of these variations is tempered in Var. 8, described by the composer as 'dolce e teneramente'. A sense of resolution or sublimation of the unrestrained rhythmic energy from Var. 7 is produced by the transformation of its rhythm in a cantabile melody (Ex. 67).

Ex. 67

Important in this variation is the rising bass line, which follows a pattern of foreshortening. Its first ascent, from C to D, occurs in the second four-bar phrase. Thereafter, in the sequences, it rises every two bars, and then finally every bar in the cadential phrase to the first half. The ascending line, and even to some extent the foreshortening, is present in Diabelli's theme—but in its melodic line. In the variation, Beethoven transfers this material to the bass, freeing the treble for a new melody.

The treble melody is a good example of Beethoven's favoured method of reshaping the melodic contours of the waltz, with its falling fourth and fifth and persistent emphasis on the dominant note G. Instead of the fifth, the third,

---

[3] This and the preceding variation are not parodies, as has been suggested by Abraham, p. 10. Their straightforward structure, virtuosity, and vigorous sentiment have nothing to do with parody, and any pointed reference to the melody of the theme is lacking.

E, frequently becomes a focal point in the voice-leading, and in this variation the third becomes the beginning of the melody itself. Beethoven's periodic recapitulations of the actual melodic contour of Diabelli's waltz stand out because his methods of variation throughout usually obliterate the initial dominant emphasis of the theme. As we shall see, this linear ambiance between G and E also plays a crucial role at the conclusion of the work.

In the second half of the variation it is the melody that ascends, and with a rich, Brahmsian harmonic tone (see Ex. 68). The minor-ninth sonority so often used for dramatic effect appears here as dark sonorous support for the melody. The variation ends quietly, with a subtle anticipation of the minor mode in the A flat of the penultimate bar.

Ex. 68

Var. 9, in the minor, together with the brilliant Presto which follows it, reach new heights of dramatic intensity, and alert the listener that this is to be a work on an enormous scale. If these variations have often been perceived as the end of the opening section of Op. 120, they represent no less a gateway to the ensuing events.

The minor variation Allegro pesante e risoluto is a masterpiece of concise, forceful, musical development. Like Var. 6, the texture at the opening is deliberately spare, to be filled out with decisive effect in the course of the variation. It is dominated throughout by the simple turn figure from Diabelli's waltz, and in the first half it also follows the theme in its ascending melodic line, now heard for the first time in the minor.

The first phrase consists wholly of turns on tonic and dominant in an ascending pattern until its last beat, when the third, E flat, is added to articulate the transition to another such phrase on supertonic and dominant. By withholding the full sound of the triad until the last beat of these opening phrases, Beethoven draws emphasis to the end of each, and after arrival at the melodic goal of E flat in bar 9, an intensification in sonority with added voices, accents, and accelerated ascent toward the dominant, completes the process of dramatic foreshortening. Heightening the effect is Beethoven's use of the three possible diminished-seventh chords in immediate succession (Ex. 69).

Ex. 69

The second half immediately counters the dominant G with the flat sixth, A flat; the ensuing passage arrives at D flat major through its dominant and through the reinterpretation of C in bar 20 as the leading note of D flat. This sets the stage for an unusually subtle interpretation of the ubiquitous seventh chord on C found in so many of the variations. When this sonority is reached in bar 24, it demands resolution not to the subdominant F, but to the neapolitan, D flat (Ex. 70). However, instead of supplying the expected resolution to D flat, Beethoven has the bass on C remain stationary, so that the music nevertheless shifts to the subdominant. And when the bass does move up to D flat, as a leading note to a tonic, the treble shifts back to notes belonging to the root C! This subtle, dialectical manipulation of the tonal equilibrium undermines the primacy of any one of these resolutions, and captures harmonic energy, giving rise to a series of implied but unstated modulations in the following bars. Beethoven even expresses these implied modulations by this notation for the bass, which alternates between D flat and the same pitch spelt as C sharp. The suspense produced by this harmonic ambiguity is finally ended when the chromatic ascent in the treble reaches A flat, and in the last bars this note, which in bar seventeen had initiated the

Ex. 70

move to the neopolitan, is resolved to C in an unambiguous linear progression from dominant to tonic.

The first 'double' of the set, Var. 10, employs written-out repetitions, and this fact clarifies the technical basis for the climactic and strongly cadential character of the variation. Its swift and brilliant sound is wedded to simple blocks of tonic and dominant harmony, and the bass pedal utilized in the repetitions underscores this harmonic framework, with its strong cadential implications. The overall harmonic scheme is shown in Fig. 6. The bass pedal in the repetition to the first half stabilizes the sway of the dominant and facilitates the modulation. Similarly, in the second half, the resolution of the pedal from dominant to tonic helps to provide a sense of finality, of cadential resolution to the tonic.

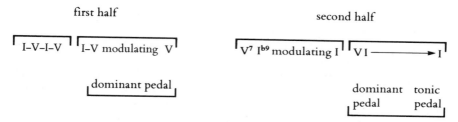

FIG. 6. Harmonic scheme of Var. 10

This variation has traditionally been regarded as the end of the first section of the Diabelli Variations, and not without reason. It is difficult to imagine how Beethoven could have avoided a caesura after this variation, imbued as it is with the utmost speed and brilliance. In fact, this Presto is unsurpassed in the Diabelli Variations for sheer brilliance. This is symbolized by the last chord alone (Ex. 71), which spans six octaves and makes any kind of registral transition, such as those which occur between most of the other variations, simply impossible. The most natural solution to the sequel was clearly a retreat to a new beginning, and this was the course actually followed by Beethoven.

Ex. 71

VIII. The Middle Variations

FROM cosmic effulgence to simplicity and grace: this is the route we follow from the fortissimo ending of the Presto to the quiet beginning (von Bülow marks it 'innocente') of the following Allegretto. Var. 11 is a kind of liquidation variation in which the turn figure from the waltz, expressed as eighth-note triplets, is resolved into sustained chord notes of a fundamental progression. In this variation, Beethoven actually simplifies the texture so that his underlying harmonic-linear scheme is revealed with special clarity. The opening phrases of the first half (Ex. 72) trace an ascent from C to E, above a sustained inner pedal on the dominant. The sequential passage, syncopated in a rather similar way to Var. 3, leads finally to a drop in the fundamental line to D at the cadence to the first half. This close is undercut rhythmically and harmonically by the syncopation and the avoidance of the leading note to the dominant; its motif is simply repeated at the lower octave to begin the second half.

Ex. 72

In this part Beethoven sometimes omits the turn in the upper voice to preserve clarity of texture, and as a result the harmonic progression is given especially lucid treatment. The minor-ninth chord on C is here composed-out horizontally, as a melodic series of thirds gradually added to the root, C (Ex. 73). This dark patch of harmony, originally highlighted as a mysterious departure in Var. 3, is wholly integrated within the overall progression of this Allegretto. In a sense, the new beginning represented by this piece corresponds with the original first variation (No. 3) but in the Allegretto we encounter, for

Ex. 73

the first time, an element of abstraction and crystallization that subtly fore-shadows the great twentieth variation.

Halm and others have pointed out that Vars. 11 and 12, like Nos. 3 and 4, are closely related, almost forming a kind of double variation based on the turn motif from the waltz. In the second of these paired variations, as in the Var. 4, Beethoven indicates a slight increase in tempo ('un poco più moto'). Furthermore, a diminution in the prevailing rhythmic value from quarter to eighth notes produces an animation in rhythm that prepares astonishing contrasts in the variations to come. In its structure, Var. 12 parallels Var. 11. Both omit repetition of the first half, and both begin the second half by restatement of the principal motif on the supertonic, just as it had occurred in the second phrase of each of these variations. In this way, the second half assumes the role of a development of material from the first half, an effect that is quite pronounced in the variation at hand.

It will be seen that the sequential passage in the first half stands in contrast to the rest of the variation in its differentiation of parts, its lack of the original form of the ostinato built on the turn figure, and its close relationship to the corresponding bars in Diabelli's theme. In these few bars, there is a departure from the more abstract tone of the rest of the variation. The reason for this discrepancy can be sought in Beethoven's compositional procedure. As we have seen, these bars were first conceived as a sequel to the first four bars of what became Var. 7, a piece of rather different character. It is interesting that Beethoven did not recompose this material when he created all the rest of Var. 12. In this case, the older material represents a kind of interruption in the ascending transpositions of the opening, and when these return, with renewed persistence, they succeed in attaining the highest register of the piano.

Then, in a marvellous stroke, Beethoven allows the ostinato to disappear, as it were, out of the highest register only to reappear in the depths of the bass, while a new voice enters in a superimposition of layers of texture (Ex. 74). This new voice, which appears as a series of syncopated chords, reaches a climax at a diminished chord on high F, which is left hanging and unresolved through the next three bars until finally, in the closing chord two octaves below, it finds resolution in the third of the triad, E (Ex. 75).

This striking linear resolution of F–E in another register provides a subtle link to the next variation, so utterly contrasting in character, for emphasis on

Ex. 74

Ex. 75

the semitone, F–E endows the sound of this third with an expectancy, and dynamic intensity. At the beginning of the next variation, two beats later, this E has become a dominant in the surprising opening chords of Var. 13 in A minor (see Ex. 75). This is an example of Beethoven's enormous sensitivity to the directional tendency of notes (or in other words, their instability), and to the interaction between linear, harmonic, and rhythmic parameters in the creation and resolution of musical energy. In the opening sonority of Var. 13, Beethoven even omits the tonic note A in the higher register in order that the continuity of the pitch E is more easily audible (in the repetition of the first half the A is of course supplied). In performance it is advisable to emphasize E in the voicing of this first chord, and it is imperative not to impose a lengthy pause between these variations, as has been suggested by Halm. (It should also be noted that due to editorial misjudgment, this opening sonority appears 'corrected'—with the upper A—in many standard editions, including that of von Bülow.)

The great comic buffoonery of Var. 13 introduces a new rhythmic dimension to the set. Though nominally in triple time, this variation creates the effect of duple metre, owing to the velocity of the tempo and the placement of strong accents in every fourth bar. The larger, superimposed rhythm of the variation is therefore that of a march, with every bar sounding as one beat in groupings of four, as Ex. 76 indicates.

This contraction in the rhythmical framework of the whole opens the door to manipulation of the total temporal mass of the thematic model, one parameter of the theme which had not yet undergone drastic alteration. The following Grave e maestoso variation in 4/4 metre contains twice as many

Ex. 76

beats as there were bars in the preceding Vivace, and this metrical expansion, in conjunction with a slower tempo, increases its relative temporal mass about threefold. After this massive slow variation, moreover, there follows a metrical compression to 2/4 time in the Presto scherzando, the shortest of all the thirty-three variations. In performance, two bars of Var. 15 will approximately equal a single beat of the Grave. The shape of the theme is thus ballooned in the slow variation, only to be most severely curtailed in the Presto, which sounds, in this context, even more fleeting than it really is. In these variations, for the first time in the set, Beethoven places each one in total contrast with the next. The most fundamental vehicle for these juxtapositions is the metrical alteration to duple time prepared by the rhythmical structure of the thirteenth variation.

There are also, of course, drastic changes in affect. The solemn procession of the Maestoso, Var. 14, is the first slow variation in the entire set, and introduces, in its breadth and measured dignity, qualities as yet unheard in the work. The contrast between this slow movement in dotted rhythms and the preceding comic parody variation could hardly be more pronounced. The Maestoso is a serious piece, even if somewhat conventional, and its spacious nobility brings the work to a point of repose which arouses our expectations for some new and dramatic gesture.

Beethoven has originally planned to follow this slow variation by the pair of march variations, Vars. 16 and 17, and evidence of this can be seen in the exact correspondence in register between the end of the Maestoso and the beginning of the first Allegro. Thus the centrepiece of the work was to have been a kind of slow, majestic overture in dotted rhythms followed by a great pair of Allegro variations which together would balance the length and weight of the overture. The character of the march variations is also majestic and statuesque, and without a trace of irony.

These variations contain as much harmonic daring as is to be found in the entire set. In the sequential bars of the second half of Var. 16, the diminished-seventh chord (crucial in so many variations) initiates a modulation to D flat major (Ex. 77). In the corresponding passage in Var. 17, the music reaches the remote tritone, F sharp major (Ex. 78). The Maestoso also exhibits imaginative

Ex. 77

Ex. 78

turns in harmony at the sequential passages in both halves and in the progression to the end of the first half, which closes in the mediant. These three
variations, therefore, display a kinship in their harmonic idiom as well as in
their affective character, and use of the conventional genre forms of overture
and march.

It is thus extraordinary that Beethoven should have separated these closely
related variations by inserting the Presto scherzando, Var. 15, between them.
This tiny, fleeting miniature was deliberately placed by the composer at the
heart of his preliminary plan from 1819, and in a sense it seems to mock not
only Diabelli's waltz, but the very structure of the variations in their original
order. The effect of hearing the Presto at this point in the set is astonishing, as
was pointed out by Yeomans.[1] However, an understanding of the special
status of this variation may help to remove one stumbling block to criticism—
the abrupt two-octave leap in the bass in the twenty-first bar.

Critics and pianists have long been puzzled by this sudden drop in register,
and have frequently attributed it to a mistake or oversight of the composer.
Indeed, on closer observation, it appears that Beethoven may have simply left
out two changes of clef—to treble clef in bar 21, and back to bass clef on the
last eighth of bar 24. This was the solution advocated by Siegfried Kross, who
amended the passage as shown in Ex. 79.[2] Alan Tyson countered, however,

[1] William Yeomans, 'Problems of Beethoven's Diabelli Variations', *Monthly Musical Record*,
lxxxix (1959), p. 12.
[2] Kross, 'Eine problematische Stelle in Beethovens Diabelli-Variationen', *Die Musikforschung*,
xvi (1963), pp. 267-70.

Ex. 79

that this emendation created another problem—the downward leap in bar 24—that is no less troublesome than the passage as it stands in the first edition.[3]

Lars Abraham, on the other hand, suggested that this capricious leap is merely a kind of 'persiflage', and that it is therefore correct as it stands. Abraham may indeed be close to the mark, in view of the strongly parodistic character of the variation, and its role as a kind of comic parenthesis between the Maestoso and the great march. As we have seen, this variation is curious in other respects, and can well tolerate oddities that would be totally incongruous in another context.

Var. 15 was evidently one of the last to be composed, since it was drafted in the Engelmann Sketchbook, on a page where Beethoven subsequently made corrections for many of the other variations. On two occasions—in this sketchbook and in the autograph of Op. 120—Beethoven wrote out the disputed passage with the leap but with no change of clef. Moreover, Beethoven supervised at least two copies of the work from the autograph—one which must have served as *Stichvorlage* for the Vienna edition, and one sent to Ries in London for the projected English edition. The latter copy has survived, and contains comments and corrections by the composer in red ink (though none of these concern Var. 15). Thus, counting the proofs for the Vienna edition, Beethoven must have written or seen this passage at least five times before it was published. If he himself viewed it as unsatisfactory, it is indeed curious that he made no change.

It is not impossible, however, that the discrepancy and perhaps even the ambiguity[4] of this passage were intentional. If Beethoven was to slight the rational ideal of logical consistency anywhere, this variation would provide the occasion. The solution to this puzzle transcends the formalistic bounds of art, as does the overall progression of the Diabelli Variations.

In the last analysis, there is something profoundly convincing about the Presto scherzando variation. Its presence contributes to our overall sense of

[3] Tyson, 'Weiteres über die problematische Stelle in Beethovens Diabelli-Variationen', *Die Musikforschung*, xviii (1965), pp. 46–8. See also Kross in xviii (1965), pp. 184–5, and Tyson in xix (1966), pp. 189–90.

[4] It is quite unusual that such a passage would admit two possible interpretations based on different clefs.

scale, and sets off Var. 16 more effectively than Var. 14 would have done. This elusive caricature calls forth the theme again, as a kind of hallucination, at that very moment in the work when drastic, bewildering contrasts have gained the upper hand. It contributes to the sense of psychological progression, to the 'logic', as it were, of the middle variations.

For theirs is a logic of dissociation.

The second of the march variations concludes with a fermata, and then finds its linear continuation in the deft strains of Var. 18. Its opening polyphonic phrase stresses the ascent to and return from the third degree, E, to the tonic, and this emphasis on E leads to a tonicization of A minor, just as occurred at the beginning of Var. 13. There is a real similarity in sound between these two passages which derives from the identical use in both of F in the high register, two octaves above the A minor triad in root position to which it seems to resolve.

Like Var. 12, No. 18 utilizes the turn derived from the waltz, and this figure, along with the motif of a third, is important throughout. The beginning of the sequential passage in the first half (Ex. 80), for example, is

Ex. 80

based on the turn from the opening of the variation, but with a lowered second, D flat. This variation exploits both the contrast between different registers and that between polyphony and homophony. Ex. 80, for example, continues in parallel octaves to the end of the first half, in contrast to the three-voice texture of the opening phrases. In the second half, the homophony gives way to two interdependent voices, but the contrast of register is heightened in such a way as to effect the long-range resolution of the remote diminished-seventh chord on D flat with highest tone E (Ex. 81). The high E in bar 24 is left hanging, suspended, and the full effect of resolution is postponed until the final unison octaves at the cadence. The abrupt drop in register at the beginning of the sequences isolates the mysterious sonority in the treble, and only bars later, as the line arches gradually upward in a four-octave ascent, does it sound the E again and carry it forth to the highest octave of Beethoven's piano, as if resolving a part of its own past.

Ex. 81

The soaring, upward motion at this cadence is abruptly countered by the headlong, canonic descent of the next variation. This Presto variation, No. 19, is in perpetual motion sustained between the close imitative exchanges of the voices. Rhythmically, it is in utter contrast with the following Andante, which is practically motionless. Beethoven's intention in juxtaposing these variations was to emphasize their difference, their polar opposition; they form a contrasting pair. In the preliminary draft for these variations, as we have seen, they were actually connected by an overlapping cadence, and in Beethoven's final solution the last bar of Var. 19 is completely filled with eighth notes, creating an urgent need for immediate continuity into the Andante. At this juncture, as at most of the other moments of transition between variations, there should be no sustained pause in performance. Arbitrary breaks between the variations only burden the listener by destroying the continuity between each variation and its larger context.

Structurally, Var. 19 is one of the most straightforward in the set. It displays little internal development of its material, and even retains the 'cobbler's patch' sequences from Diabelli's theme. In Beethoven's variation, however, the upward motion from the waltz is continued, ascending a full octave to E before the cadence. Perhaps the finest moment of the variation occurs in the final four bars, where the head motive in canon returns unexpectedly, and with a driving impetus sustained to the last imitative exchange in the last notes. Then, from the roughly angular, rhythmical world of this Presto, we enter a world of contemplative vision and emotional abstraction which represents a landmark in the structural organization of the entire set.

In this great enigmatic slow variation, No. 20, we have reached the still centre of the work. With all rhythmic energy withdrawn, the voice-leading and sheer sound of the chords is paramount. The canonic texture of the opening (Ex. 82) enables Beethoven to bring attention to the conflict between A natural and A flat, which is of crucial importance. In the closing bars (Ex. 83), the bright and open sound of the A natural returns, leading to what

Ex. 82

Ex. 83

seems as a momentary flash of illumination before the reappearance of the A flat at the final cadence. The strangest moment in the variation, and *a fortiori* in the whole work, is contained in the sequences of the first half. In the first bars of the section Beethoven writes chromatic chords in which, as Uhde puts it, 'motives from the theme seem to be solidified into crystal'.[5] But immediately following this, in the bars marked pianissimo, this chromatic voice-leading is abandoned. The diminished-seventh chords that follow seem not in any strict sense to be resolved at all (Ex. 84). Close examination of this passage reveals, however, that they are indeed eventually resolved within the larger progression to G major. A linear reduction of these bars is shown in Ex. 85. The chords in bars 11–12 are unrelated to each other, but are integrated into a larger context because they belong to independent, superimposed linear progressions joined at the following tonicization of G. The passage is not

---

[5] *Beethovens Klaviermusik*, vol. I, p. 542.

Ex. 84

Ex. 85

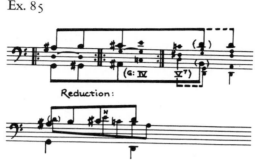

chaotic, but it gives the effect of startling, discontinuous juxtaposition. The tonic chords following the diminished-sevenths, though eventually resolved as IV of V, sound neither familiar nor stable, but instead remote and mysterious. The very straightforward harmonies in the following bars are bathed in the aura of this progression. In this passage, and in the variation as a whole, the familiar appears transfigured, detached, and aloof from action. Here we have reached, perhaps, the citadel of 'inner peace'.

This atmosphere is crudely shattered by a grotesque parody of the theme mollified by the minor strains of the Meno Allegro in Var. 21. In this variation, finally, the increasingly drastic contrasts between successive variations are embodied even within the internal structure of a single piece. It is as if the polar contrasts of Vars. 19 and 20 admitted a sequel of even greater—and now internal—disunity. There is, therefore, a certain logic of succession even within discontinuity in the Diabelli Variations. After Var. 21, however, this disjunctive logic of succession recedes in importance. The Janus face of this variation marks the extreme limit of the progression toward dissociation that had begun about ten variations before.

An even more important effect of this variation, however, is to mark a turning point after the other-worldly vision of the Andante. And in this sense, its rhetorical significance as a parody of the theme and gesture towards a transcendence of it is paramount. After this variation a new sense of parody is evident, not merely as caricature of the theme, but as the evocation of styles and idioms that absorb an almost encyclopaedic range of contexts, historical and contemporary. Towards its close, the subject of the Diabelli Variations ceases to be merely the waltz, or even its possibilities of formal transformation, and becomes the entire musical universe as Beethoven knew it.

The drastic juxtaposition of Vars. 20–1 represents, then, a point of articulation in the progress of the entire cycle. Following it are a series of evocative parodies, beginning with the allusion, in the unison octaves of Var. 22, to 'Notte e giorno faticar', from Mozart's *Don Giovanni*. In devising this variation, Beethoven is reputed to have been grumbling at all his hard work in composing the Variations,[6] but even if true, this story touches only one dimension of the parody. The allusion is brilliant not only through the musical affinity of the themes—which share, for example, the same ascending fourth and fifth—but through the reference to Mozart's Leporello.

This is because Leporello shares a psychological trait usually developed to a considerable degree by great artists—a capacity for ironic detachment. A quotation from Leporello fits the work whereas a quotation from the Don, or virtually any other character from the opera, would not: Beethoven's relationship to his theme, like Leporello's relationship to his master, is critical but faithful. And like Leporello, his variations now gain the capacity for disguise, as if they were not what they seem to be. With uncanny wit, this variation expands the scope of the set beyond the formalistic limits of art.

After 'Notte e giorno faticar' most of the variations belong to the later period in composition. This is true for the next three variations, and each of these pieces, in a different way, follows the trend toward psychological complexity established by the Mozart parody. Var. 23 is a kind of parody of an étude for piano in which technical dexterity outweighs musical expression. This pretence of busy virtuosity allows Beethoven to poke fun at the static opening phrases of this waltz by filling these bars in his variation with pianistic gestures at once ostentatious and harmless. After a full-voiced tonic chord in the first bar, the rest of the first phrase consists of a threefold repetition of sequences built on the turn and organized in two voices, much in the manner of a piano exercise. The second part of each half is based on syncopation between the hands, another standard idiom of the étude literature.

We can discern the frame of reference for Beethoven's allusion as the famous *Pianoforte-Method* by Johann Baptist Cramer and most specifically, to its very first study. A comparison of the openings of both pieces is shown in Ex. 86. The rhythm, spacing of the opening chord, and similarity in the sequences of sixteenth notes confirm this relationship. It is fitting that Beethoven, in this great encyclopaedic piano work, should have paid his respects to Cramer, who was the only contemporary pianist he admired. In a

[6] This story appears, for example, in Martin Cooper, *Beethoven: The Last Decade 1817–1827* (London, 1970), p. 208.

Ex. 86

broader sense, of course, Var. 23 also represents a parody of pianistic virtuosity in general. It might even be regarded as a proleptic parody of another contributor to Diabelli's collection—the twelve-year-old Franz Liszt!

Var. 23, the Cramer parody, is a companion piece to the Mozart parody. Both share the same time signature, and lack an upbeat to the first bar, and though they are wholly distinct in character, subtle musical parallels exist between them. In the second half of each, for example, there is a pronounced emphasis on the pitch E, the third of C major. In Var. 22, Beethoven even added a bar at the point when the motive appears on the pitch level of E (see Ex. 87), in order to gradually change the mode from E major to minor in

Ex. 87

preparation for the return to C. At the analogous passage in the next variation, a tonic seventh chord is treated as an augmented sixth, resolving to an E minor chord, and E is then stressed as a kind of upper pedal in the treble (Ex. 88).

With the close of this virtuosic piece, we encounter yet another of those drastic juxtapositions which have been practically consistent since Var. 14. A Fughetta follows, 'una corda, sempre ligata', a smooth, lyrical piece not at all typical of Beethoven's essays in fugal writing in his other late instrumental works. Uhde describes the atmosphere of this Fughetta as 'simultaneously

Ex. 88

cool and warm; as like a phenomenon of nature and yet much more than a symbol for that; as consolation, solace; as serious and objective and full of love'.[7] These words come close to the description of a religious phenomenon. In fact, the closest and only parallels to this Fughetta in Beethoven's other works are certain quiet devotional passages in the *Missa Solemnis*, and more obviously, the Fugue in the last movement of the Sonata in A flat, Op. 110.

This sonata, written in the autumn of 1821, is bathed in the aura of the Mass, and the concluding Fugue assumes a dimension which might almost be regarded as religious in nature. The last movement of Op. 110 begins with a searching, impassioned recitative which yields to the despairing Arioso dolente in A flat minor. The Fugue takes its origin from the earthy pain of this lament, but its smooth, ascending line, consonant harmonies and inward strength bring consolation, and at the end of the work, after a return of the arioso, a kind of ecstasy. The musical language of this Fugue, moreover, has much in common with the Fughetta from Op. 120. In both works, the use of suspensions, conjunct motion and avoidance of accent help build energy within the music which raises the emotional temperature of every phrase. This atmosphere also permeates the Praeludium to the Benedictus and other passages in the Mass. Indeed, it is hard to imagine how Beethoven could have composed this Fughetta in the Variations before his work on the *Missa Solemnis*.

An important dimension of the Fughetta is its archaic atmosphere, which in counterpoint and rhythm reaches back to the idiom of J. S. Bach. Its continuous rhythmic flow in eighth notes divided among the voices follows baroque precedent, and its consonant thirds and sixths also sound archaic in this context. They are certainly not typical of Beethoven, and they do not sound it.

They sound in fact more typical of late Bach, and Beethoven's assimilation of the music of Bach was most probably an inspiring force behind the Fughetta.[8] This kinship is revealed more clearly if we compare Beethoven's

---

[7] Uhde, p. 545.

[8] Beethoven's reference to Bach in Vars. 24 and 31 has been discussed in general terms by Martin Zenk, 'Rezeption von Geschichte in Beethovens "Diabelli-Variationen," Zur Vermittlung analytischer, ästhetischer, und historischer Kategorien', *Archiv für Musikwissenschaft*, xxxvii (1980), pp. 61-75.

variation with Bach's second small 'Kyrie Gott Vater in Ewigkeit' for organ (Ex. 89), from the *Clavierübung*, III, for example. Bach's work, like Beethoven's, involves free fugal treatment in four voices (in this setting, only the first notes of the chorale are used to suggest the thematic material), and is parallel to Beethoven's in metre, key, and in its characteristic use of suspensions (such as in bars 5–6 above). In addition, Beethoven's variation is written in an idiom that suggests the organ. Most of all, however, it is the intensely sublimated atmosphere of this late work of Bach, quite apart from the similarity in musical language, that implies the source of Beethoven's homage.

Ex. 89 Kyrie. Gott Vater in Ewigkeit. Alio modo. Manualiter.

The emotional fervour of the melodic lines of the Fughetta, however, is uniquely Beethovenian. The upper line, in particular, seems sometimes to strain upwards as if towards an invisible force, only to sink back again. This melodic urgency first appears during the last of the fugal entries, as the soprano presses to E and then, more briefly, to F (Ex. 90). In the analogous passage in the second half, the longest-breathed passage in the variation, the highest voice reaches high G and then high A before sinking back in a series of sequences (Ex. 91).

Ex. 90

Ex. 91

This variation is also notable for its extraordinary economy of material. The subject itself consists of a descending fourth or fifth and rhythmic augmentation of the turn figure from the waltz, while the countersubject grows out of a freely adapted form of the same turn figure in eighth notes. The greater intensity of the second half flows naturally from the inversion of the fugue subject, and the use of harmonic progression through minor keys. Then, to lead from the end of these minor sequences, Beethoven employs a free treatment of the head of the subject in the bass, supplying the I–IV–V progression in root position in the tonic C major with a consequent purity of sound and poignancy of effect that is unforgettable (Ex. 92).

Ex. 92

Why did Beethoven place the Fughetta at this point in the work, and what role does this variation play in the overall form? As in the case of Var. 20, Beethoven juxtaposed with the Fughetta variations of utterly contrasting character; there is no direct continuity between it and its neighbouring pieces. That is not to say, however, that it is an isolated character piece placed arbitrarily into the set. It extends the series of parody variations that precedes it by its evocation of the archaic and by its sublimated spirituality; it seems bound neither by the time frame of its composition, nor by its medium of performance. This image from the past—suggesting, perhaps, an organ prelude from a hundred years before—foreshadows a crucial aspect of Beethoven's final evolutionary progression in the last nine variations of the work. And the Fughetta, in the hushed expectancy of its close, is also a highly effective curtain for the signal event that follows it: Var. 25, the last and most humorous of the parodies, which turns Diabelli's waltz into a fumbling Ländler.

At this point we should pause to assess the formal role of the middle variations of Op. 120. Is there some unifying equivalent of larger sections or movements that embraces groups of these variations? This is a question that has preoccupied numerous critics and analysts, including von Bülow, Halm, Geiringer, Uhde, Porter, Butor, and Münster.[9] The results of their studies,

---

[9] Hans von Bülow, notes in his edition of Op. 120 (New York: Schirmer, 1926), pp. 56, 70, 76; August Halm, *Beethoven* (Berlin, 1927), p. 177; Karl Geiringer, 'The Structure of the Diabelli Variations', *Musical Quarterly*, l (1964), pp. 496–503; Jürgen Uhde, *Beethovens Klaviermusik*, vol. I

however, have been equivocal and even contradictory where they concern the middle variations. We have already seen the inadequacy of the schemes advocated by Geiringer and Butor. Nearly all the other analysts see the first ten variations as an opening section, but they are in substantial disagreement about the organization of the variations that comprises the large central section of Op. 120.

August Halm, the first scholar who dealt at length with the Variations, perceived four sections in this part of the work, Vars. 11–12, 13–17, 18–21, and 22–4. These can be reconciled at least partly with Porter's scheme, which consists of Vars. 11–17 and 18–23, and assigns the Fughetta to the beginning of another section. Of these two plans Halm's seems the more convincing; Vars. 11 and 12 are in fact closely related, and some kind of kinship holds between Nos. 22, 23 and perhaps even 24 (they are all parody variations). It is difficult to see, however, how Vars. 13–17 or 18–21 form a group in at all the same sense as Nos. 11–12, or even 1–10. And it is even harder to follow Porter in grouping Vars. 18–23. Why one grouping and not another?

Von Bülow solves the issue more simply, placing a 'grand division' after No. 10 and again after 23, on account of the extreme virtuosity of these variations. Uhde, on the other hand, advocates a group spanning Vars. 11–20, which he calls a 'group of contrasts', as the second section of a scheme depicting the outlines of a four-movement 'Variation Symphony'.[10] (Vars. 21–8 represent, in his scheme, a 'scherzo group with trio, Var. 24'.) About the presence of contrasts, and powerful ones, there is no question. But what is problematical in his, and in these other studies, is the specific variation groupings. It is doubtful that any of these schemes imply either internal closure and coherence, or unambiguous demarcation between adjacent sections, as between movements of a sonata work, for example.

The recent analysis by Münster is equally unsatisfactory in this regard. Guided, like Geiringer, by a predisposition to seek hidden symmetrical structural plans, Münster advocates a problematical grouping encompassing Vars. 11–19, a grouping similar to that advocated by Uhde, but containing one fewer variation, nine instead of ten.[11] Münster is at pains to discover divisions containing precisely nine variations, since according to his analysis the larger structure of the work should consist in four groups of nine variations each, comprising Vars. 2–10, 11–19, 20–8, and 29–33. Since the last of these sections contains fewer than nine variations, Münster is compelled to argue that these represent the 'equivalent' of nine, with the Fugue standing in place of five variations, although it is shorter, in performance time, than some of the

(Stuttgart, 1968), pp. 554–5; David Porter, 'The Structure of Beethoven's Diabelli Variations Op. 120', *Music Review*, xxxi (1970), p. 298; Michel Butor, *Dialogue avec 33 variations de Ludwig van Beethoven sur une valse de Diabelli* (Paris, 1971), pp. 33–8; Arnold Münster, *Studien zu Beethovens Diabelli-Variationen* (Munich, 1982), pp. 166–72, 175, 195.

[10] Uhde, pp. 554–6.

[11] Münster, p. 175.

preceding single variations.[12] In this case, concern with the notion of structural groupings becomes an obsession, revealing more about the a priori conceptions of the analyst than about the musical organization of the work itself.

Yet if we reject such schemes as artificial, we need not fall into the position of Maynard Solomon, for whom the Variations most resemble 'a gigantic cycle of bagatelles'.[13] It is only necessary to reflect that the extreme diversity and contrast between the successive variations, which reaches its climax in Var. 21, may itself play an important role in the form of the work. Significant in this connection is the fact that very little tonal contrast is utilized by Beethoven; only the penultimate Fugue leaves the tonality of the tonic major or minor. In the absence of sustained modulation, this work still achieves a sense of large-scale contrast through the diversity of variations in its middle section. The extremity of contrasts can be gauged by Beethoven's juxta-position of the three slow variations (Nos. 14, 20, 24) with three swift parodies, Vars. 15, 21, and 25. Contrast is practically axiomatic towards the centre of this immense work.

It is tempting to venture an analogy with sonata form, or the kind of psychological progression embodied in the sonata style. Standard procedure in this style is to maximize contrast towards the centre of the movement, and to consolidate the form beginning at the recapitulation, approximately two-thirds of the way through. Once liberated from the compulsion to obscure the contrasting character of the middle variations by the imposition of artificial groupings (or analogues to the four-movement sonata, as Uhde's 'Variation Symphony'), we can see that Op. 120 consists of one large form with three distinct regions. The opening variations remain close to basic parameters of the theme (such as its metre) and show gradually increasing freedom, which at last turns into dissociation toward the centre of the work, in increasingly radical juxtapositions.

Throughout this central region, however, a sense of progression is evident, not only toward differentiation, but toward abstraction, epitomized in the Andante, Var. 20. Vars. 21–4, passing beyond abstraction, reaffirm the concrete by absorbing a set of external contexts from the world, still seemingly disjointed. And then, out of this landscape of contrast, in a way reminiscent of the remarkable Presto scherzando variation, the theme returns, again.

[12] Münster, pp. 167–8.   [13] *Beethoven*, p. 305.

IX. Consolidation and Transfiguration

In the twenty-fifth variation, the naïve simplicity of the theme makes its last appearance as a distorted German dance, and this event marks the beginning of the inevitable consolidation of the overall form. In the fore-going variations, extremes meet to an extent that is unparalleled in Beethoven's music, and the effect of each variation is enhanced by its dissociation from context. There are, to be sure, internal relationships that hold between these variations, and there is a definite psychological progression projected in them; the variation order is not chaotic or unplanned. But it is precisely the impression of chaos, of enormous, bewildering contrasts, that defines the formal role of these middle variations in the entire work. Beginning with the thematic parody in the twenty-fifth variation, the successive variations again begin to cohere, and to point in the same direction.

The means by which this cohesion is achieved is one of the most significant but misunderstood features of the Diabelli Variations. Careful examination of the four variations beginning with the waltz parody reveals, however, that they are intimately related as members of a series. In fact, it is doubtful that either Var. 25 or Var. 28 can be justly appreciated if they are divorced from this context, since they are in a sense less autonomous than most of the other variations. Their individual integrity is subordinated to their role in the overall progression.

In his preliminary draft, Beethoven had entered only one of these four variations, No. 27, but in the finished work it became the basis for a group of pieces united by a musical technique that exercised special fascination for the composer in the early 1820s. This technique—a series of progressive rhythmic diminutions—is of course a venerable device in the long history of variation writing, but it was never used more effectively than in a cluster of Beethoven's late piano works.

The first example from these years can be found in the sixth variation of the finale in the Piano Sonata, Op. 109, from 1820. In this variation, the theme is recapitulated in its original shape with the accompaniment of a dominant pedal which begins at the speed of the theme, but is then gradually accelerated in a series of five diminutions until it becomes a pulsating trill sustained through the remainder of the variation. Another example, the Bagatelle in C major, Op. 119, No. 7, from 1822, achieves its climax by an analogous treatment of rhythmic diminution above a pedal sustained as a trill in the bass.

(This bagatelle is of special interest here since it seems to be a spin-off from the Diabelli Variations.[1]) Moreover, in another work composed in 1822, the Arietta from the last Piano Sonata, Op. 111, Beethoven found means to apply this technique on the level of an entire movement. In the Arietta, each variation prior to the cadenza-like passage in E flat introduces diminutions from the preceding variation, and in the recapitulation and coda these rhythmic layers are synthesized and superimposed.

Each of these pieces uses diminution of rhythmic values as a primary means of achieving intensification in expression. It is perhaps not surprising that Beethoven found use for this practice at precisely that moment in Op. 120 where he sought means to connect a series of variations leading forcefully and irrevocably away from the parodied image of the waltz in Var. 25.

In the Diabelli Variations, in contrast to these other examples, the effect of the progressive rhythmic intensification is not contemplative or exploratory, but dramatic. In four stages, a surrogate for the waltz is presented, gradually transformed, and finally obliterated by the sheer blind energy which is the outcome of foreshortening of rhythm and accent. The culmination of this process, in turn, generates energy that makes possible a transition to the set of slow minor variations, and hence to the conclusion of the entire work. The rhythmic progression in the four variations beginning with the last thematic parody (Vars. 25-8) is thus a keystone in the overall structure, and it has not only formal but dramatic and indeed almost programmatic implications. None the less, it is precisely these variations that have been least well understood, and most often inadequately performed. The reasons for this are worth pursuing in detail.

The main problem concerns the unusual notation used by Beethoven to express the rhythmic transition from Var. 25 to Var. 26. He omitted a separate tempo indication for the latter—the only instance of such an omission in the whole set—and carried over the 3/8 metre from the preceding variation, even though this does not conform to the phrasing of Var. 26, which consists invariably of two groups of three sixteenth notes. This variation is thus actually in duple metre, in 6/16. Why, then, should Beethoven have continued with 3/8 metre, and suppressed a new tempo indication? The obvious answer, that the tempo and length of bars in these two variations should be approximately equal, is almost certainly correct.

Critics, however, have tended to discount this notation on the grounds that a slowing in tempo is needed after the 'Allegro' of Var. 25,[2] and in fact the latter variation is usually given such swift performance that later slackening of the tempo is inevitable. One suspects, though, that this overly-fast tempo is primarily motivated by musical considerations. Pianists tend to be un-

[1] See Edward Cone, 'The Late Bagatelles: Beethoven's Experiments in Composition', *Beethoven Studies*, ii, ed. Alan Tyson, p. 85.
[2] See, for example, Uhde, p. 546.

comfortable with this variation, not realizing that it is a parody and is deliberately distorted, and as a result it is usually performed much too fast. In fact, it is slower than the 'vivace' of the theme, although it is written in 3/8 bars instead of 3/4 (the theme, for that matter, is also often played too fast, so that it no longer sounds like a waltz). A faster tempo will of course mitigate the clashes in the bass with the treble at the beginning of the bars, but these should be emphasized—they are part of the joke. The strangeness of this piece must be accepted at face value. If it is not, a keystone in the structure of the work collapses. The structure of no other work of Beethoven's hangs on so fragile a thread.

The rhythmic relations between these four variations can be described as follows. The waltz parody has one strong beat per bar throughout, and this is emphasized by the accompaniment and by complete lack of any syncopation such as occurs in the theme. Var. 26 has two pronounced beats per bar, the first of each group of sixteenth notes. In Var. 27 this pattern is further subdivided into three distinct beats per bar, articulated by sixteenth–note triplets. Finally, the climax of this process is reached in the drastic rhythmic foreshortening of Var. 28, in which the music is telescoped into 2/4 bars containing systematic collisions between accents and dissonances, and staccato articulation of every chord. The rhythmic basis for the progression is shown below:

Var. 25 3/8

Var. 26 3/8 (6/16)

Var. 27 3/8

Var. 28 2/4

This increasing agitation of rhythm is paralleled by an increase in dissonance. The relatively consonant strains of Var. 26 are whipped up in Var. 27 by dissonant appoggiaturas exploited in all registers and with considerable virtuosity. The process is taken still further in Var. 28, in which a dissonant chord, usually a diminished seventh, is placed on every strong beat throughout. Intensification in the frequency and strength of dissonance proceeds from one appoggiatura chord per bar in passages of Var. 26 to three in Var. 27 until, at the beginning of Var. 28 (see Ex. 93), the diminished-seventh sonority and its resolution monopolize the entire content of the music.

The final Allegro from this series contains music quite as relentless as any to be found in the Fugue of the 'Hammerklavier' Sonata, or the *Grosse Fuge*. It is meant to be harsh, and should not be underplayed in performance. The point of this variation is precisely its effect of uncontrolled blind energy, which, having gradually grown out of the thematic parody, finally obliterates all

Ex. 93

traces of its origin. After this catharsis, we move into a new world of sound beyond, a transfigured world, in which the most direct ties to the waltz, and to the world it represents, are permanently severed.

The enormous rhythmic momentum generated by the relentless collisions of accents and dissonances in Var. 28 enabled Beethoven to devise a transition from it to the first of the trilogy of slow minor variations. The close of the Allegro is abrupt, and the silence following its last tonic chord is filled with aftershocks from its driving rhythm. Then, in a brilliantly simple stroke, Beethoven begins the Adagio without an upbeat on the melody note G, the fifth of the tonic triad. As a result, the C chord from the cadence to the Allegro sounds as the upbeat to the beginning of the slow variation (see Ex. 94). This linear connection exploits the crucial descending fourth C–G from the theme as an audible thread of continuity into the slow movement, miraculously spanning the abyss between the polar disparity of these variations.

Ex. 94

The last five of the Diabelli Variations expand the possibilities of the work beyond anything Beethoven envisioned in the spring of 1819. The original 'minore' in the early plan became a set of three slow minor variations; sketches for a fugue subject were expanded into a lengthy triple Fugue; and the Finale and coda drew upon material from the great variation movement that concludes Beethoven's last sonata for piano, composed in 1822. Moreover, a new sense of historical consciousness and vision now permeates the musical progression. The last variations seem to recreate the course of musical history, from Bach to Beethoven's own Op. 111.

Beethoven's music from this period is rich in historical references beyond itself. The outstanding example is the *Missa Solemnis*, which shows the evidence of Beethoven's studies of much sacred composition from the sixteenth and seventeenth centuries,[3] and his assimilation of the traditional rhetoric of mass composition. The greatest historical strokes in the Mass, however, do not rely upon assimilation of tradition, but on the bold juxta-position of different idioms. For his setting of the 'Incarnatus est', Beethoven revived the Dorian mode, yet moments later, at the words 'et homo factus est', the music shifts into D major and the warmth of tonality. This passage derives power not only from the remote ethos of the distant past, but from our sense that the later idiom is actually an advance, that the birth of tonality is itself capable of dramatizing the birth (or rebirth) of mankind. In other archaizing passages in the Mass and in the G major section of the Ninth Symphony Finale there is often no sense that these historical references are superseded, as in the Credo of the Mass. But it is significant that the conclusions of both works stress an immediacy of experience that leaves all such references behind. The end of the Mass, in particular, in its 'depiction of inner and outer peace',[4] is highly subjective, though without a trace of sentimentality.

In the great keyboard works from these years, Beethoven tends to make archaizing references to Bach. In the transition passage from the slow move-ment to the Fugue in Op. 106, for example, the third interlude is an evocation of the contrapuntal idiom of Bach which is broken off after a few bars. Its role is to point toward the creation of a new contrapuntal style, in the ensuing Fugue, that supersedes the fugal idiom of Bach.[5] In the Diabelli Variations, there is reference to Bach in three pieces, the Fughetta and the first and last of the slow minor variations—the two which are late in composition. What is more, these archaizing references do not end with Bach. In the Fugue, the repeated notes from Diabelli's waltz are infused with rhythmic verve and treated sequentially, in a manner reminiscent of Handel. Following the Fugue, the elegance of Mozart comes to light in the stately Minuet. Most extra-ordinary of all, Beethoven's own Op. 111 becomes the subject of the coda. With the ironic detachment of a great solitary, Beethoven surveys in Op. 120 the whole compass of musical history that most mattered to him, including his own contribution to that history.

There is another reason why Beethoven should have recalled the Op. 111 Arietta at the close of this work, one that concerns the intimate interrelation-ship of their genesis. The nature of this relationship can be clarified from the evidence of the sketches; it is by no means an insoluble mystery, as Münster

[3] See Warren Kirkendale, 'New Roads to Old Ideas in Beethoven's Missa Solemnis', Musical Quarterly, lvi (1970), pp. 665–701.

[4] Beethoven's original inscription in the autograph of Op. 123 used the word 'Darstellung' ('depiction'). Beethoven subsequently changed the inscription to 'prayer for inner and outer peace'. The passage in question, with the original words 'Darstellung der inneren u. äusseren Frieden' is found on p. 203 of the manuscript Artaria 202, Staatsbibliothek preussischer Kultur-besitz, West Berlin.

[5] See Rosen's discussion in The Classical Style, pp. 427–8.

has recently claimed.[6] The theme of the Arietta seems to have been influenced by Diabelli's waltz and Beethoven's preoccupation with it, as can be seen by a comparison of the two,[7] shown in Ex. 95. As Uhde has pointed out, the motivic and intervallic parallels between these themes could scarcely be accidental. However, the differences are also striking. In the Arietta, there are no sustained tonic and dominant harmonic areas at the outset; the material on tonic and dominant that comprises half of Diabelli's first variation half is

Ex. 95

[6] p. 211.
[7] This comparison is presented in Uhde, p. 504, in a somewhat different form.

telescoped, in Op. 111, into only one quarter of the first half of the theme. Although the Arietta follows the intervallic structure of the waltz closely, it does not follow Diabelli's proportions, which give undue emphasis to static blocks of harmony, with monotony of effect.

The Arietta theme was of course not begun as a kind of variation on Diabelli's waltz. In its early sketches it began not on C but on G, while the waltz is nowhere in evidence. Still, all of these early sketches show a dance-like character in 3/8 metre akin to the world of Op. 120 (the chorale-like setting in 9/16 appears only in advanced sketches). Also, it is interesting in this connection that Beethoven was obsessed, while sketching the Arietta, with the opening of its theme. In his detailed study of these sketches, William Drabkin observed that 'The most striking feature of the Arietta sketches is that most of them are concerned only with the first few bars'.[8] A representative example from these sketches is shown in Ex. 96, in Drabkin's transcription. Subsequently, after prodigious sketching, Beethoven adopted the opening fourth and fifth which also appear in the waltz (see Ex. 97). It seems safe to surmise that Beethoven was influenced by the project which had occupied him so intensely almost three years before but was still unfinished.

Ex. 96

Ex. 97

If the Diabelli project left its mark on Op. 111, the latter was to leave a much deeper mark on the final variations of Op. 120. For a major innovation of the Diabelli Variations is the manipulation, in several of the last variations, of the proportions of the original waltz. In each case, the opening bars of the waltz, which are harmonically static, are telescoped into half the number of bars they would normally occupy. And in each case in which this occurs—in Vars. 29, 31, and 33—the pieces were written after the completion of the Arietta of Op. 111. In this sense, the direct structural model for these late variations is not Diabelli's theme at all, but Beethoven's own last piano sonata. In this light, Beethoven's extensive reference to Op. 111 in the Minuet and coda of Op. 120 looms still larger and more significant. These exalted

[8] See William Drabkin, *A Study of Beethoven's Opus 111 and its Sources* (unpub. Ph.D. diss., Princeton, 1977), vol. I, pp. 178–80, and vol. II (transcriptions), pp. 36–8.

variations are in a sense a continuation of the creative deed of the famous Arietta.

In view of these internal relationships, and the complex interdependence of these pieces in Beethoven's creative process, the claims advanced by Butor[9] as to the special significance of the number of thirty-three variations, though at first startling, cannot be dismissed. (Butor makes his case on general grounds, without knowledge of the complex relation between these works.) The Variations include, at their culmination, a kind of postscript to Beethoven's thirty-second sonata, and the thirty-third variation is explicitly indebted to the last sonata. Although Beethoven generally showed little interest in hidden puzzles and symbolic meanings, this temptation would perhaps have been too hard to resist.[10]

The first of the Op. 120 variations to transform the proportions of the theme in ennobling it is the Adagio ma non troppo, Var. 29. In this piece, placed at the beginning of the trilogy of minor variations, the first two bars of the variation correspond to the first eight of the theme; after that point, one bar of the variation corresponds to two of the theme. On this more compact structure, Beethoven writes a kind of Baroque lament on a very simple harmonic scheme, in which each bar of the first half alternates between tonic and dominant (Ex. 98). This harmonic simplicity, in the minor, adds to the

Ex. 98

bleak, austere sadness that characterizes the variation, and provides a gradual point of departure toward the increasingly chromatic texture of the next two variations.

This Adagio is the second of three variations in the set that refer to Bach, and as in the Fughetta, we can observe a relationship here to a specific work of the older master. This time it is to the E flat minor Prelude from Book I of the

[9] Butor, pp. 33–8.

[10] It may not be a complete coincidence, furthermore, that Beethoven wrote thirty-two variations, one fewer than in Op. 120, in his C minor Variations, W080, of 1806.

Well-Tempered Clavier, a piece which, in texture and sentiment, is strikingly parallel to the Adagio ma non troppo. This extensive reference to Bach seems fitting in light of the fact that the only comparable variation work to Op. 120, in scale and magnificence, is the Goldberg Variations, and as we shall see, the last and most touching evocation of Bach is indeed to this masterpiece, in the great Largo, Var. 31.

Var. 30 was the original 'minore' from the preliminary draft, and features of its structure and texture differ considerably from its two neighbouring variations composed in 1823. Unlike them, this Andante follows the structural proportions of the theme, although in 1823 Beethoven did add an element of asymmetry by omitting the repetition of the first half altogether and repeating only the last four bars of the second. The texture is polyphonic and chromatic, and the harmonic scheme is biased toward the Neapolitan, D flat. Much of the variation, in fact, is not in C minor but in D flat major, the first half closing in A flat. The function of the second phrase in the second half is to modulate back to the tonic from the Neapolitan, and this is achieved in a passage of haunting beauty, quoted in Ex. 99. The ethereal serenity of this variation is due partly to its Neapolitan chromaticism, to the bright but remote sound of D flat major in relation to C minor. This tonal ambiguity undermines the sense of finality at the close of the variation, raising our expectations for a continuation after the fermata on the last chord.

Ex. 99

The great Largo, Var. 31, again shows the influence of Bach. Charles Rosen has characterized this variation as 'an imitation of the ornamented minor variation of the Goldberg'.[11] That Beethoven knew the Goldberg Variations has not been documented, but melodic and textural similarities are sufficient to imply that he did, though of course the relationship suggests less an imitation than an homage to Bach. The very beginning of each variation, for example (Bach's Var. 25 and Beethoven's Var. 31) is based on a melodic descending minor sixth (Ex. 100). At the end of each variation half, Beethoven's descending closing motive bears a striking resemblance to Bach's (Ex. 101). Moreover, Beethoven follows Bach in his florid texture in which important melody notes are stressed by an upward leap, usually of an octave.

[11] Rosen, p. 439.

Ex. 100   Beethoven, Op. 120, Var. 31, opening

Bach, Goldberg Variations, Var. 25, opening

Ex. 101   Beethoven, Op. 120, Var. 31, bar 5a

Bach, Goldberg Variations, Var. 25, bar 31

In the face of this internal evidence, it is difficult not to assume Beethoven's familiarity with the Goldberg.

This Largo is a kind of grand aria-variation, in which intricate, almost improvisatory ornamentation adorns the melody. The single melodic tone A flat in the third bar, for instance, generates an arc of sound traversing the interval of a tenth (Ex. 102). At the beginning of the second half (see Ex. 103), Beethoven expresses the ascending sixth derived from the waltz as an even faster melodic diminution, which sounds the entire tonal space from G to E flat, including all of the chromatics, in a way presaging Chopin. Beethoven preserves the most characteristic intervallic features from the theme, but disguises them under the mask of decoration that makes the ever-familiar seem new. The closing motive of the variation is, for instance, just an ornamented form of the fourth (or fifth) from the waltz, compressed into a single beat (Ex. 104).

Ex. 102

Ex. 103

Ex. 104

In its modulatory scheme, the Largo foreshadows the tonality of the following Fugue by its move to the relative major, E flat, at the beginning of the second half, and by its abbreviation of the tonic area immediately before the actual transition of the Fugue. Only the final bar of the second half is in the tonic, and even this arrival is undercut by Beethoven's omission of a bar at the end of the variation. This shortening of the second half is the result of Beethoven's last compositional decision—not to extend the trills after they reach the dominant note of the tonic triad in the final bar. The composer may have felt that there was no feasible way to continue this exalted progression after the gradual chromatic ascent in the bass, which had begun two bars before, reached the fifth of the tonic. To the strains of the closing motive, the variation overflows its last bar in a brief transition to the dominant of E flat major, the key of the ensuing Fugue.

The subject of the Fugue utilizes the descending fourth and repeated notes of the waltz, but here they are for once not the object of travesty. Instead they are endowed with Handelian breadth and Beethovenian energy. After two bars of urgent repetitions on the dominant, the subject continues with a sequential descent to the third, reinforced by complementary motion in the countersubject (Ex. 105). This is an inversion from the ascending sequences of the theme. The almost constant presence of these thematic motives in the Fugue provides it with an important synthetic function in which the head of the waltz melody, although immediately recognizable, is entirely abstracted from the banality of its original context.

Ex. 105

This variation in fugue is a highly ambitious piece, and a rare example in Beethoven's works of a triple Fugue. Three strongly contrasted subjects are combined at the climax. The third subject is introduced after a dramatic pause on a diminished-seventh chord (Ex. 106). Its motion in eighth notes is then combined with the quarter notes of the main subject and the half notes of the countersubject. This occurs for the first time at the last return of the tonic E flat major, with a grand and exciting effect (Ex. 107).

Ex. 106

Ex. 107

The Fugue is the first piece in the entire set in a key other than the tonic major or minor, although some others, notably the two immediately preceding variations, had modulated extensively. It is noteworthy that the modulatory scheme of the Fugue avoids its own dominant B flat, but emphasizes C minor, the relative minor of E flat and the tonic minor of the entire work. After the opening fugal exposition in E flat, a brief transition leads to C minor for a second exposition of entries, and then eventually to F minor and other keys before a return is made to E flat at the beginning of the third exposition. After this section ends the third subject appears in E flat but tending toward its subdominant, A flat. Then, following the exposition of the third subject, a one-bar transition leads to F minor, and it appears that another exposition will occur in the key until a sudden entry of the principal subject brings back the tonic E flat for the final exposition that is to combine all three of the subjects at once.

The most important tonalities of the Fugue are thus E flat major and its subdominant, A flat; and C minor and its subdominant, F (the subdominant emphasis derives from the answer to the fugal subject in IV, a common procedure in Beethoven). These are all keys related to C minor. Just as stress on E flat major in the Largo anticipated the key of the Fugue, so does the emphasis on C minor in the Fugue render the E flat modulation less conclusive, preparing the return of the tonic major in the Minuet finale. It is partially by these means that Beethoven could maintain a sense of continuity through these variations to the C major conclusion, and weaken the sense of autonomy of the pieces immediately preceding the finale. This anticipatory use of tonalities is schematized in Fig. 7.

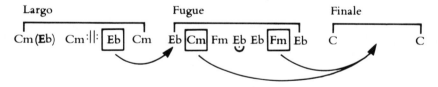

FIG. 7. Beethoven's use of tonality at the end of Op. 120.

The most salient characteristic of the Fugue as a whole is its propulsive, rhythmic energy, generated from the strong accents and repeated notes of the subject. Nevertheless, this rhythmic tension is not discharged in the Fugue itself, which is devoid of strong downbeats at the end of the subject, where a series of syncopations often deflects an impending sense of cadential resolution. Instead, the rhythmic resolution of the subject itself is withheld until its final appearance at the end of the Fugue, and this sets the stage for one of the most magical moments in the work, the transition from the E flat Fugue to the final Minuet in the tonic C major. When the final appearance of the subject in the subdominant leads, for the first time, beyond the subject to a structural downbeat, the dominant diminished-seventh chord (the one so important in so many variations) becomes the crucial sonority to receive this downbeat, the strongest in the entire work (Ex. 108). Beethoven emphasizes the diminished-seventh chord by a kind of arpeggiated cadenza spanning four and then five octaves. When the music comes to rest on this dissonant sonority, it is clear that we have reached the turning point, and are poised at a moment of great musical import.

Ex. 108

What accounts for the power of the following transition, which has so impressed musicians and critics? (Tovey called it 'one of the most appallingly impressive passages ever written'.[12]) One reason is surely the sheer temporal weight of the thirty-two variations that precede it, lasting three-quarters of an hour in performance. At this moment, there is finally a halt to the seemingly endless continuity of variations in an unprecedented gesture. But this still fails to explain the uncanny force of the chord progression modulating from E flat major to the tonic C major of the Finale. The course of this modulation seems to transfigure a musical relationship that has become very familiar, to modify the expected in an unexpected way.

For the diminished-seventh chord with highest note C flat is the same sound, in relation to the key of E flat,[13] that had served as a climax in the tonal structure of many variations in C. But here, for the first and only time in the work, the minor ninth (C flat) does not simply resolve downwards to the fifth of a new triad; or at least it does not seem to so resolve. Instead, after the expected harmonic resolution is once given, there is a return to the C flat with a subtle shift in harmony, and eventually a linear resolution *upward* to C (Ex. 109). This effectively purges the effect of the minor ninth. It is transformed at last into a leading note, so that the pure consonances of the Minuet resolve, unambiguously, the harmonic complex which throughout the set had

---

[12] Tovey, p. 133.
[13] Here, however, it is a diminished-seventh chord with dominant function to the tonic E flat. In the rest of the work, the diminished seventh is built above the tonic C, and resolves to the subdominant.

Ex. 109

been a primary source of dissonance. If Beethoven's pervasive use of the diminished-seventh chord supporting D flat had weakened the tonic, by turning it into a dominant of the subdominant, this final culminating resolution greatly strengthens it. It clears the air for the final affirmation of the tonic major in the last variation.

Another striking aspect of the transition lies in its unexpected shift to an E minor triad, mediant of C, by the enharmonic reinterpretation of E flat as D sharp. Nor is this merely a colouristic shift without broader implications: in many variations, as we have seen, Beethoven had stressed the mediant of C, especially as a focal point for the linear structure. The move to E at the threshold of the Finale and the imminent return of the tonic has, however, a still more cogent relation with Beethoven's coda, and the final moments of the work.

Immediately following, we hear a kind of final spiritualized reminiscence of Diabelli's country dance as a Minuet, with all the grace of the classical minuets of Mozart (Ex. 110). The first part of this Minuet variation also recalls the 'Tempo di Menuetto' style of the first movement of Beethoven's Piano Sonata in F major, Op. 54, from 1804.[14] More lies behind this Finale than an evocation of the classical Minuet, however. There is a striking parallel with Mozart's *Don Giovanni*, the work already cited by Beethoven in Var. 22. At the

Ex. 110

[14] For a discussion of Beethoven's use of the 'lyrical Minuet' in these and other works, see Harry Goldschmidt, *Um die Unsterbliche Geliebte* (Leipzig, 1977), pp. 283–93.

beginning of the Finale to the second act of the opera, Mozart cites a series of popular tunes from other operas, from Martín y Soler's *Una Cosa Rara*, Sarti's *I due Litiganti*, and finally from his own *Marriage of Figaro*. These excerpts, played by the band on stage, provide the pretext for humorous commentary by Leporello, who remarks that the tune from *Figaro* sounds 'very familiar'. *Don Giovanni* had of course been written for Prague in 1787 after the success of *Figaro* a year earlier: Mozart's witty allusions to *Figaro* could hardly have been missed by the original audience. It is remarkable how closely Beethoven follows this procedure towards the conclusion of the Diabelli Variations, where, however, Beethoven alludes to the styles of other composers rather than quoting them directly, as Mozart did. As in *Don Giovanni*, there is a series of allusions to other composers leading ultimately to the self-quotation of a work written a year earlier: in Beethoven's case the Arietta of Op. 111. Furthermore, there is an additional point of contact between the Variations and *Don Giovanni* at the beginning of the Minuet finale, which betrays a definite kinship to the opening of the famous G major minuet from the Finale to the first act of the opera. Beethoven's reference to *Don Giovanni* is thus much more extensive and profound in nature than is implied by the parody of 'Notte e giorno faticar'. It is in the context of this elaborate parody of Mozart and the historical vision embodied in the last variations that we may view the most fascinating relationship of all: how Beethoven's own last piano sonata becomes the subject of the coda.

Here, just as with the parody of Mozart, the relationship is more than merely melodic or rhythmic: it is structural. Even at the beginning of the Minuet finale, the Op. 111 Arietta is very near at hand. In this variation, as in Vars. 29 and 31, Beethoven foreshortens the proportions of the first bars of the waltz, thus making the melodic parallel with the Arietta more evident. Furthermore, the system of rhythmic diminutions that underlie the sonata movement is reflected in the Minuet, though in a compressed and somewhat altered form. In the first four bars of the Finale, the prevailing motion is in quarter notes (strictly speaking, eighth notes plus eight rests). The first diminution occurs in the following sequential bars, where the prevailing motion is in eighth notes. Subsequently, in the next two bars, it reaches sixteenths, and finally triplet sixteenths in the penultimate bar. Each half of the Minuet is based upon three successive diminutions in the rhythm, reaching a climax in the bar before the cadence.

Moreover, the last of these diminutions provides a springboard for yet another, realized in the coda, at the moment that Beethoven recalls the texture from the mysterious fourth variation from the Arietta. The parallel with the Arietta is striking, as can be seen by a comparison of the rhythmic diminutions in each work:

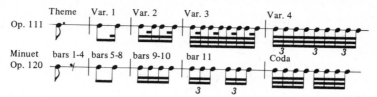

This is, however, only one aspect of the affinity between these two pieces. Another is motivic. The opening three-note figure of the Minuet (see Ex. 110 above) is very close to the Arietta, and in the coda, when Beethoven recalls this motive in imitation, the kinship amounts almost to quotation (see Ex. 111). This passage in Op. 120 is the beginning of the last of three concluding half-variations, which strive to perpetuate the repetitive momentum of the theme.[15] In these closing bars the system of rhythmic diminutions, culminating in thirty-second notes is recapitulated, and in these final diminutions, it is the descending fourth, so crucial in both works, that is highlighted.

Ex. 111   Op. 111

Op. 120

But we have not yet touched on the most intimate relation between Op. 111 and Op. 120, one which has to do with the entire structure of the coda in the Variations, and its affinity with the fourth variation in the Arietta. The coda consists of three half-variations of eight bars each, with an extension of two bars at the end of the first half-variation:

1st half-variation (8 bars) + 2 bars extension (10 bars)
2nd half-variation (8 bars) Begins with reference to beginning of second half of Op. 111/II, Var. 4
3rd half-variation (8 bars) Begins with reference to Op. 111/II, coda

[15] Compare Tovey's comments on Beethoven's variations in the last pages of his unfinished *Beethoven* (London, 1945).

The purpose of the extension is to absorb rhythmic force from the syncopated, emphatic arrival at the upper C in the previous bar where a sudden, dissonant collision with the tritone F sharp in the bass contradicts, with a shock, our expectations for a tonic cadence. A series of syncopations descending an octave leads finally to the expected cadence three bars later, at the beginning of the second half-variation, the one that recalls the intervallic suspension utilized in Var. 4 of the Arietta. Here, as we have seen, the interval suspended is the major third C-E, a relationship foreshadowed in the transition to the Finale.

At this point it is important to reassess the rhythmic preparation for the analogous passage in the last sonata, for it is not only Beethoven's suspension of the interval of the minor sixth high above the unsounded bass that makes it so effective. No less important is the rhythmic impact of the A minor cadence on the strong beat beginning the second variation half after a long series of syncopations, in which the melody notes are consistently placed off the main beat (see Ex. 112). The cumulative tension generated by these syncopations is at last released at the cadence, and this event seems to cause the rhythmic animation of the arabesques in the highest register after the cadence. The series of pulsations in the upper line arises, as it were, from the long-denied articulation of the structural downbeat.

Ex. 112

Beethoven approximates this same effect in the corresponding passage in Op. 120 (Ex. 113). The powerful dissonance on the second beat of the third bar of the example creates a sudden disorientation in rhythm analogous to the long-range effect in the Arietta.

What is more, Beethoven brings back the syncopation at the end of the third half-period, in the last chord of the coda of the Variations (Ex. 114). At this moment, the rhythmic relations from the beginning of the coda are reversed: the last of the series of rhythmic diminutions leads to the syncopated

Ex. 113

Ex. 114

chord, which had previously prepared those diminutions. At the same time, the first dissonant syncopated chord at the beginning of the coda audibly prepares the last chord at the end of the coda.

Like the end of the *Missa Solemnis*, the close of the Diabelli Variations is ambiguous, and pregnant with implications. It ends, essentially, in the middle of the thematic structure, poised before an open door, a door which leads, if it leads anywhere, into the midst of the Arietta of Op. 111. So it is that Beethoven drew upon the substance of the last movement of his last sonata in completing the final section of the Variations, his last extended work for piano.

We have been able to perceive a unity of intention behind all of Beethoven's later additions to the Diabelli Variations. By inserting a series of parodistic variations recapitulating the melodic contour of the theme, Beethoven imposed a larger scaffolding over the whole set, and established a significant relation between the theme and the huge edifice of variations. Following the last thematic parody, moreover, a remarkable series of interconnected variations obliterates and then transforms the theme into the most contemplative of slow movements, and the most etherealized of Minuets before an end is reached close to the ecstatic vision of the famous Arietta from

Op. 111. This framework—projecting the metamorphosis and transfiguration of the commonplace waltz upon which the whole set is founded—was absent from the early plan. The overall structure of the Diabelli Variations bears, as has been said, an intimate relation with the story of its genesis.

Beethoven's last word, however, is still another step removed from his evocation of Op. 111. The same chord that was the peak and goal of Diabelli's theme—a C major triad with highest note E—is the surprising final sonority of Beethoven's Variations. The unresolved linear tension embodied in this chord is a reminder that Beethoven's work is one of created, not congenital, harmony, and that in these closing bars we have reached, in the words of Thomas Mann's character Kretzchmar in *Dr. Faustus*, 'an end without any return'.

PART III: TRANSCRIPTIONS OF THE SKETCHES

X. Preface

THE two central documents in the genesis of the Diabelli Variations—the reconstructed Wittgenstein Sketchbook, and the Paris-Landsberg-Montauban Draft—are transcribed below in their entirety. Whereas the other sketch sources could be adequately discussed with the aid of musical examples in the text, the scale, complexity, and chronological significance of Wittgenstein and the PLM Draft warrant complete transcription. These sources provide the reader with a rare opportunity to glimpse into Beethoven's workshop at a formative stage of one of his greatest works.

The transcription presented here is not of the 'diplomatic' type, which employs a minimum of editorial additions and emendations. To facilitate reading and intelligibility, editorial clefs, rests, and accidentals have been added, enclosed by brackets. Time signatures have not been supplied editorially since they are generally self-explanatory, but dotted lines have been used as editorial barlines and ties. Where notes have been emended, the original reading is shown by means of underlined letters next to the emended notes. Doubtful readings are shown by question marks. In addition, many of the sketches have been supplied titles, enclosed by brackets, that identify their contents.

Some features of the 'diplomatic' transcription are, however, retained. The direction of the stems of the notes follows the original. Most important is the distribution and spacing of the music on the page. In Wittgenstein, the spacing of the sketches is frequently a function of their musical relationship and their order in composition. In the Draft, on the other hand, the relation between the music and its format is the means by which we can conceptually restore the missing portions of Paris 77A and Montauban. Beethoven's brace-lines at the left-hand margin have also been retained. They are significant because they sometimes disclose his intention to draft an entire variation which is fleshed out only in part.

Beethoven frequently returned to his sketches to revise them and add new material in the space that remained. Where this occurs in Wittgenstein the later entries are marked off by asterisks. The first drafts in Paris 77A, on the other hand, contain three layers of superimposed writing. In the first draft it was possible, working from the original, to reconstruct the first layer; two independent transcriptions are provided for this draft. For the second draft this proved impossible because of the illegibility of the first layer. Here only the composite transcription is provided.

The transcription of the reverse of the Montauban fragment was made on location at the Musée Ingres in Montauban, France. The director of the museum, M. Pierre Barrouse, kindly permitted removal of the sketch from its frame. It was then necessary to gingerly lift the bottom of the manuscript to enable the transcription to be made; the top of the fragment is glued to a board which it shares with two other sketchleaves, by Haydn and Mozart. The present dimensions of the leaf have been indicated in the transcription. The original manuscript was on 16-stave paper, but the bottom stave was cut away together with two-thirds of the length of the leaf when it was mutilated and put on display in 1840.

The Wittgenstein Sketchbook has been published in facsimile and transcription, edited by Joseph Schmidt-Görg.[1] The reader is referred to this edition, and to the authoritative review of it by Robert Winter.[2] Its facsimile is an indispensable means of evaluating the present transcription, which, like most sketch transcriptions, is inevitably interpretative. Unfortunately, as we have seen, the Bonn edition omits the two Paris leaves. I am of course indebted to Schmidt-Görg's published transcription. There are, however, substantial differences between it and the present transcription, both in the musical reading and in the identification of sketch material. In the latter respect Schmidt-Görg is notably conservative, identifying material relating to no more than ten of the finished variations. In the present transcription, partly as a result of the inclusion of Paris 77B, material relating to as many as twenty variations is identified.

A basis for many of the following transcriptions is work of the late Dr. Erich Hertzmann, Professor of Music at Columbia University. During the ten years before his death in 1963, Hertzmann made transcriptions of these sources, excluding the Montauban fragment, which he evidently did not know. At the time of his death, these materials passed to Prof. Daniel Heartz at the University of California, Berkeley, who reconstructed some of Hertzmann's work on these sketches for a paper which was presented to a meeting of the American Musicological Society at Santa Barbara, California, in May 1963. Prof. Heartz also revised and corrected Hertzmann's transcriptions of the Paris leaves, which are provisionary and sometimes incomplete. With characteristic generosity, Prof. Heartz showed these transcriptions to me at an early stage in my own study of the Diabelli Variations.

I have made further revisions in these transcriptions, and have supplemented them to some extent with additional material. Study of the original manuscripts in Europe has enabled me to make refinements in the transcription of difficult passages, particularly in Paris 77A and the Wittgen-

[1] *Ein Skizzenbuch zu den Diabelli-Variationen und zur Missa Solemnis*, SV 154, ed. Joseph Schmidt-Görg (Bonn, facsimile, 1968; transcription, 1972).
[2] *Journal of the American Musicological Society*, xxviii (1975), pp. 135–8.

stein Sketchbook. For the first page of the autograph, which is in private hands, I relied upon photographs supplied to me by the Beethoven–Archiv in Bonn.

XI. Transcriptions

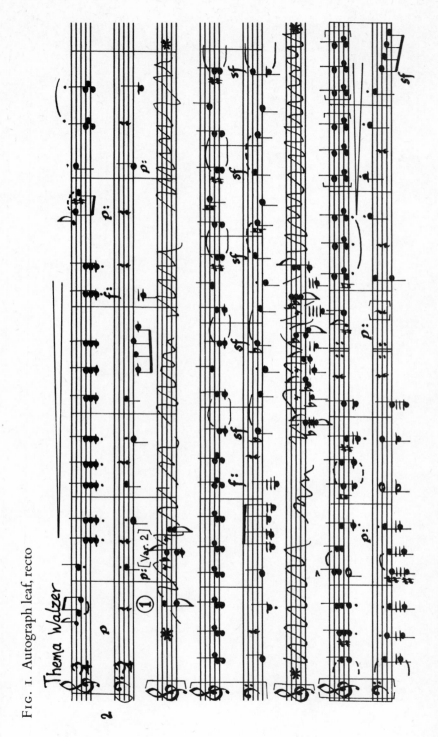

FIG. 1. Autograph leaf, recto

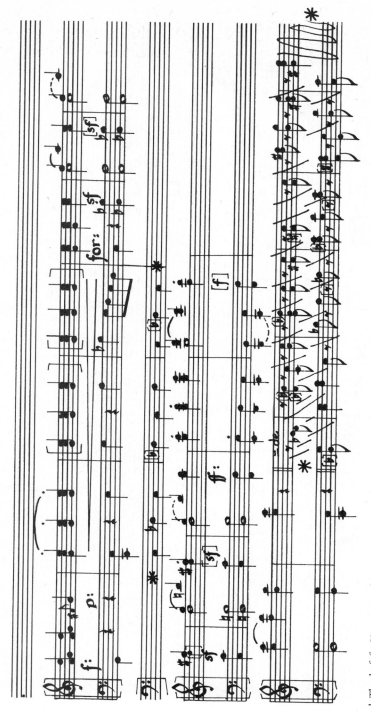

¹ The draft for Var. 2 entered beneath the corresponding bars of the theme derives from Beethoven's late period of composition, in 1823, and has been enclosed by asterisks. Most of the draft was crossed out by Beethoven, and parts of it are totally illegible. Much of the character of the draft is revealed, however, by the four passages that permit transcription.

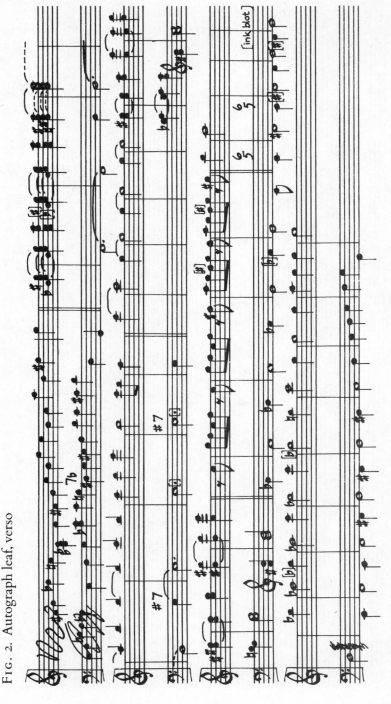

FIG. 2. Autograph leaf, verso

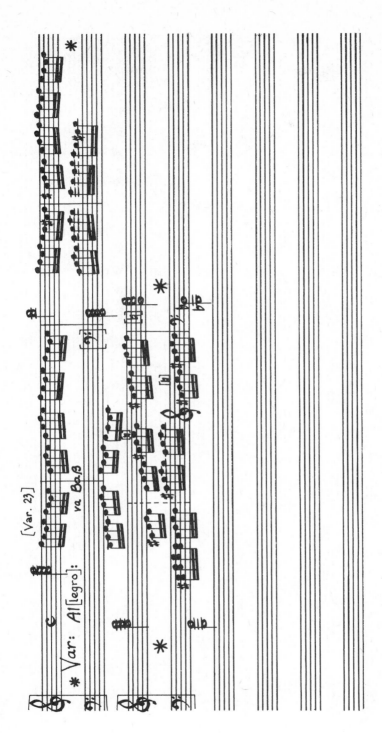

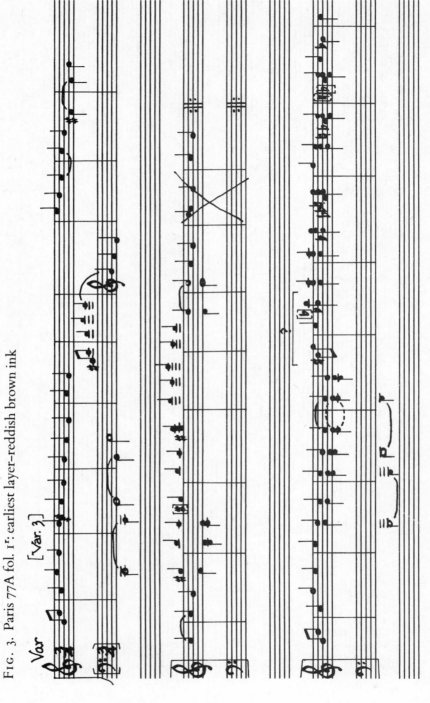

F IG. 3. Paris 77A fol. 1ʳ: earliest layer–reddish brown ink

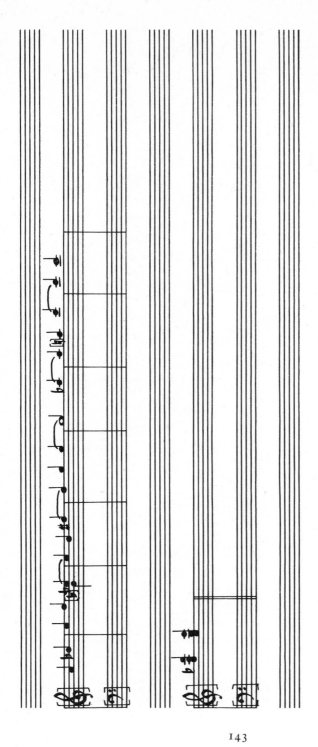

FIG. 4. Paris 77A fol. 1^r: latest composite layer[2]

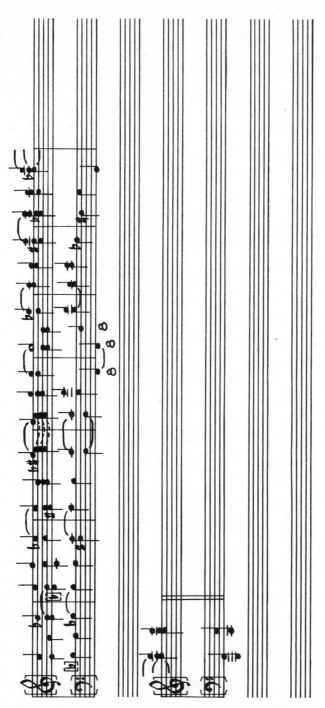

¹ The number '1' (−1), in Beethoven's hand, shows that there could have been no other drafts, now lost, preceding the present draft for Var. 3.

² In this and the following draft, not all of the visible sketches are transcribed, since these drafts have been written three times. In the interest of intelligibility, composite transcriptions are provided which seem to represent Beethoven's latest level of composition.

Fig. 5. Paris 77A fol. 1v: latest composite layer

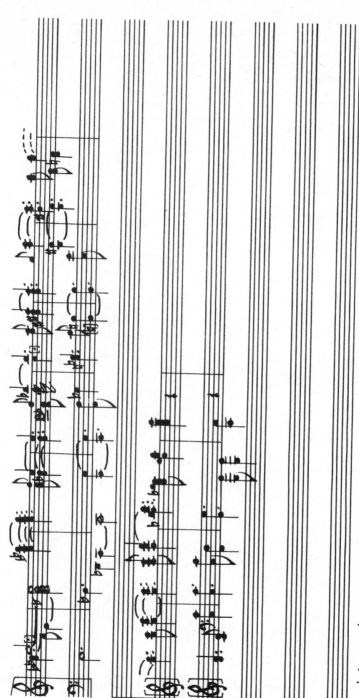

[1] An extra beat is contained in this bar.

FIG. 6. Paris 77A fol. 2ʳ

V:7 Assai Viv[ace]   [Var. 9]

FIG. 7. Paris 77A fol. 2ᵛ:

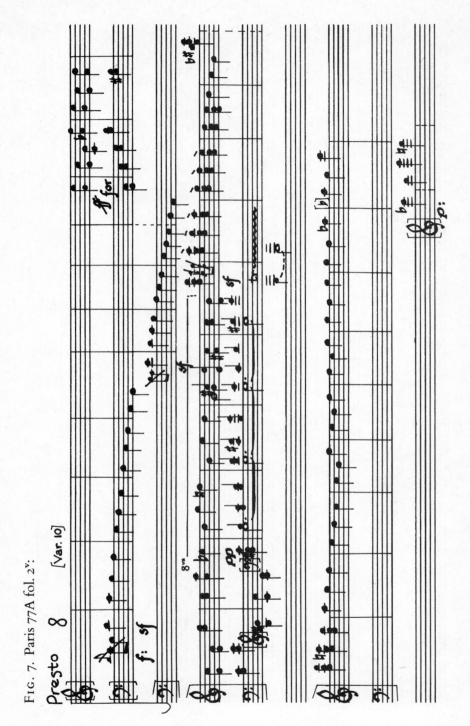

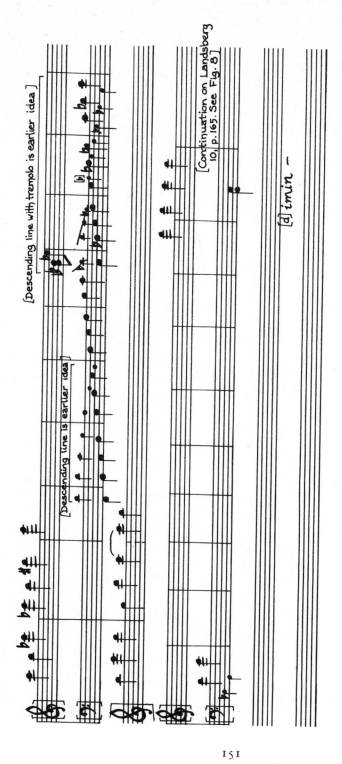

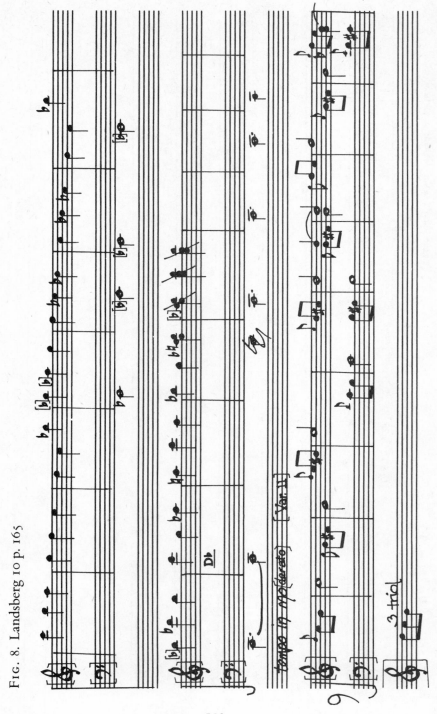

FIG. 8. Landsberg 10 p. 165

153

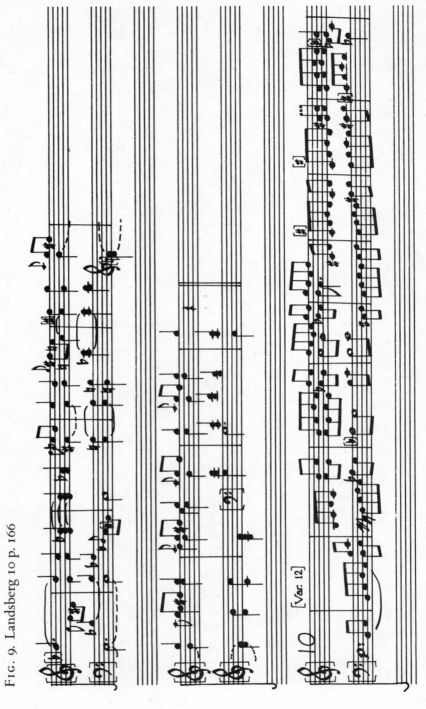

FIG. 9. Landsberg 10 p. 166

154

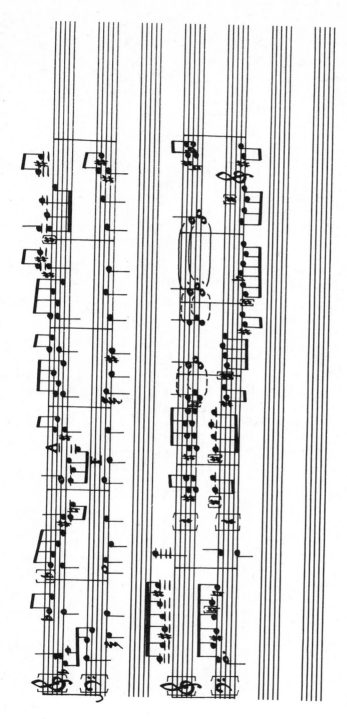

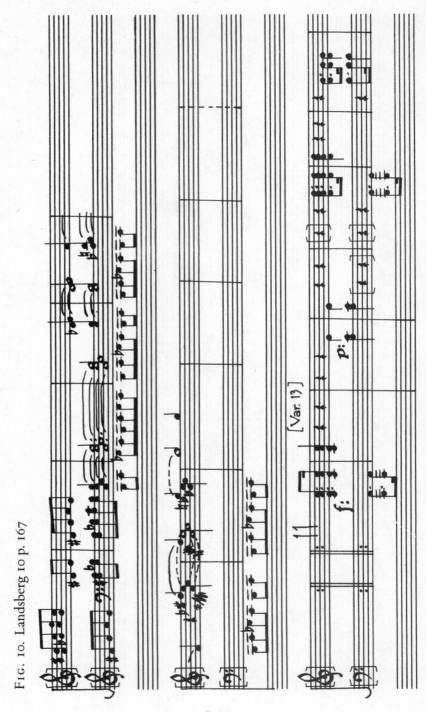

FIG. 10. Landsberg 10 p. 167

156

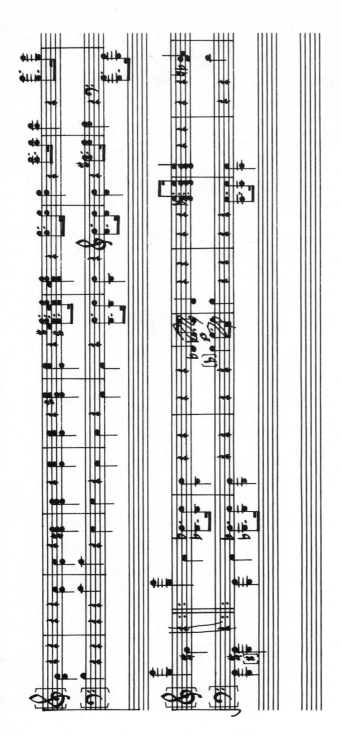

157

FIG. 11. Landsberg 10 p. 168

FIG. 12. Landsberg 10 p. 169

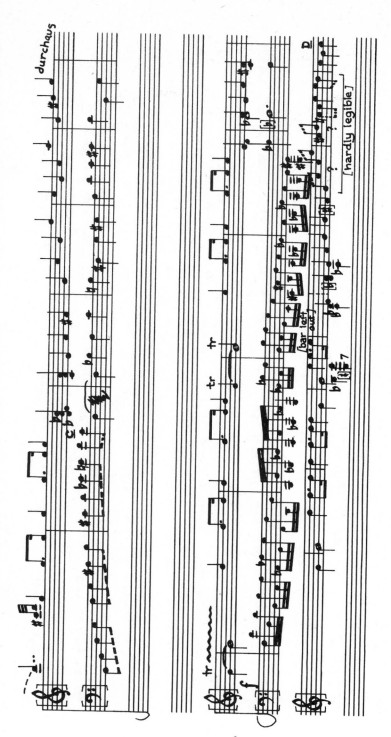

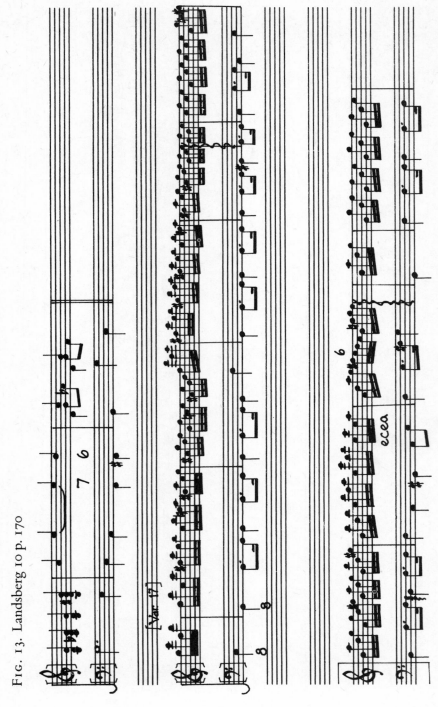

FIG. 13. Landsberg 10 p. 170

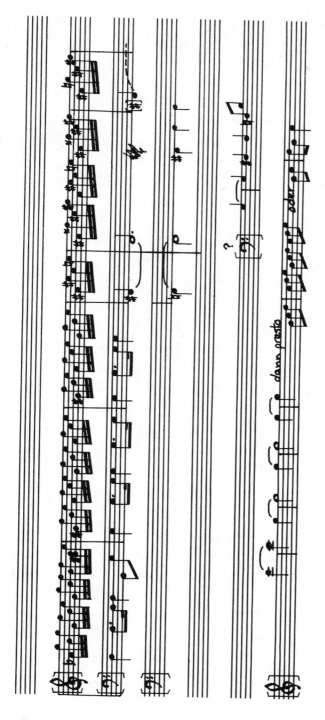

163

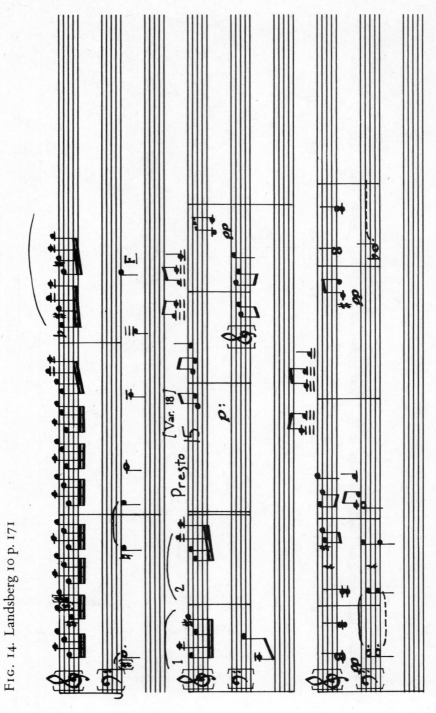

FIG. 14. Landsberg 10 p. 171

164

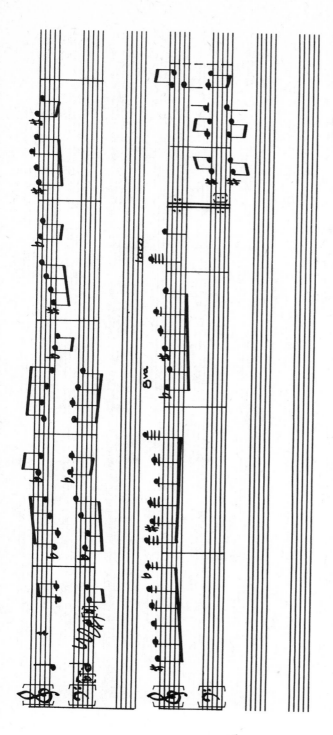

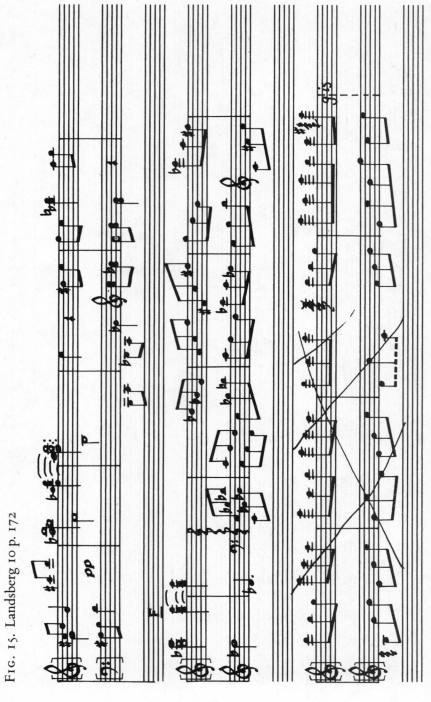

FIG. 15. Landsberg 10 p. 172

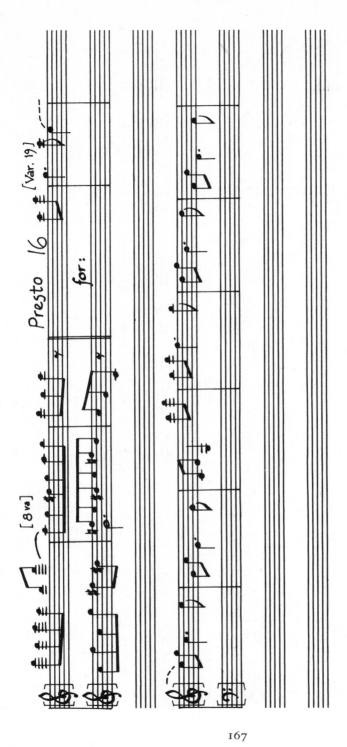

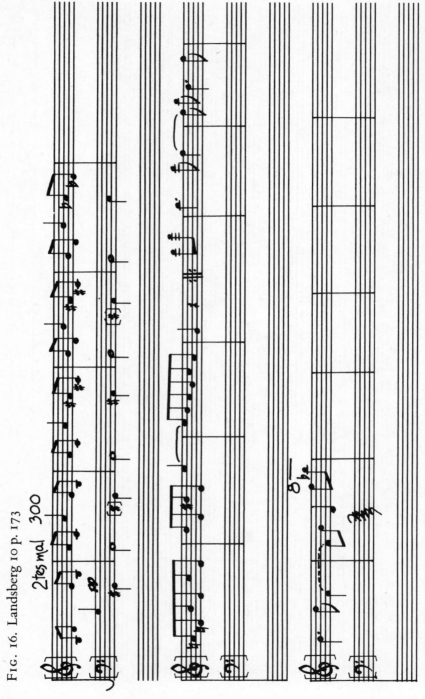

FIG. 16. Landsberg 10 p. 173

169

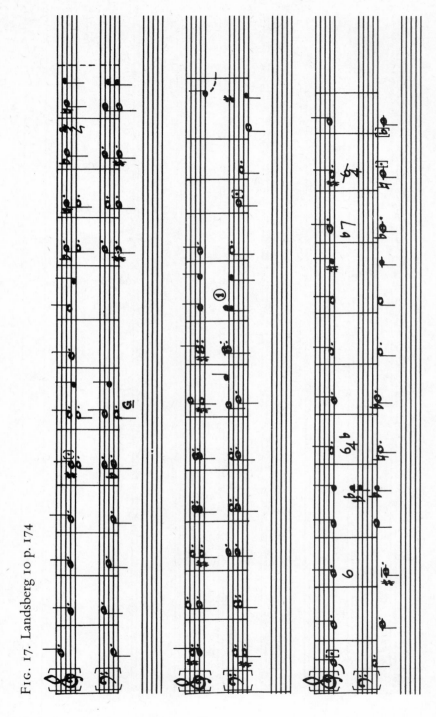

FIG. 17. Landsberg 10 p. 174

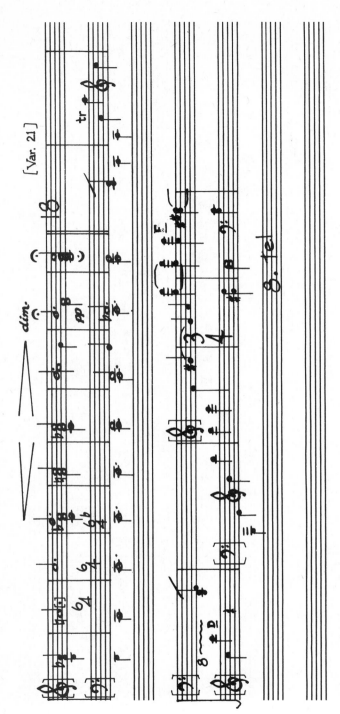

[Var. 21]

[1] One beat is missing in this bar.

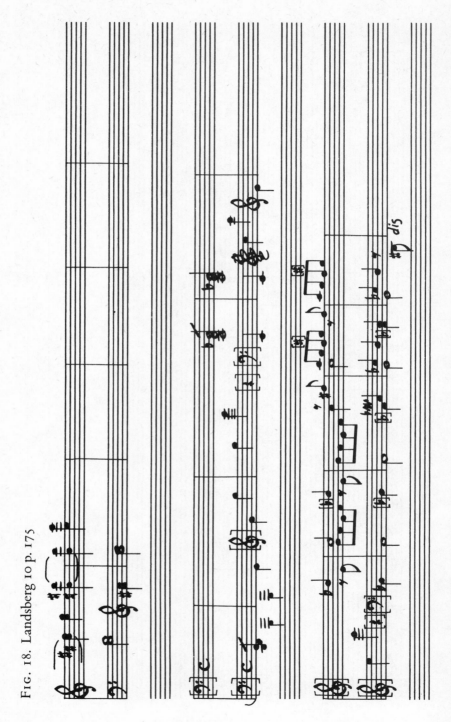

FIG. 18. Landsberg 10 p. 175

172

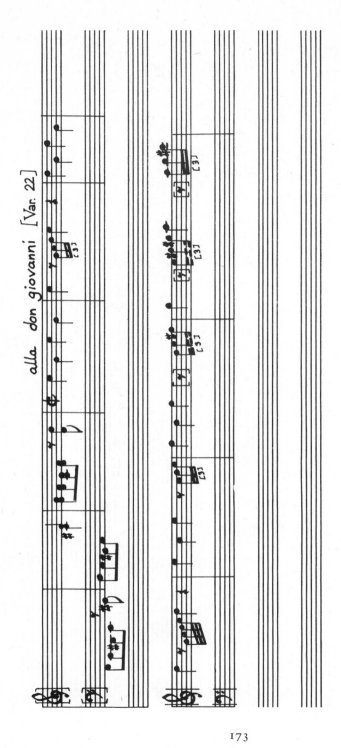

alla don giovanni [Var. 22]

FIG. 19. Landsberg 10 p. 176

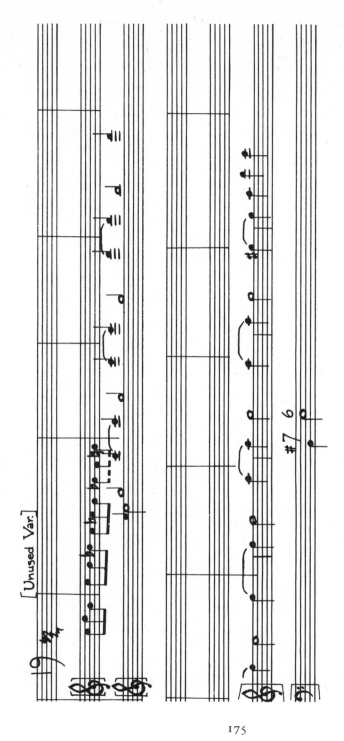

175

Inscription on top of cardboard holding all three MSS:
'Manuscrits

de

Haydn   Mozart   Beethoven

Donnés à L. D. Besozzi par M. le professeur Franz Hauzer

[Vienne 1840]'

Then, below the MSS:

'Offerts respectueusement à Monsieur J. Ingres par L. D. Besozzi ancien pensionnaire de l'Académie de France à Rome'

The present dimensions of this leaf are 123 mm × 196 mm

FIG. 20. Montauban Fragment, recto

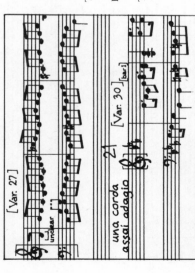

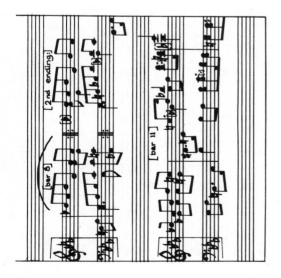

FIG. 21. Montauban Fragment, verso

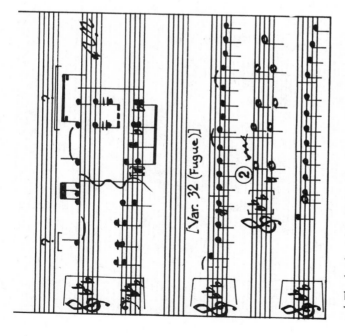

[Var. 32 (Fugue.)]

[1] The sketches in the third and fourth systems represent a transition from the slow minor variation to the ensuing Fugue. Beethoven evidently considered fore-shadowing the principal subject of the Fugue by the repeated G motif sketched at the end of the first bar of the fourth system. His plans for this transition are thus reminiscent of the 'largo' which introduces the Fugue of the 'Hammerklavier' Sonata, written in 1818.

[2] These entries seem to represent two independent sketches for the countersubject of the Fugue.

FIG. 22. Wittgenstein Sketchbook fol. 3^v

[Draft for Var. 18, 32 bars (beginning)]

[Continued on fol. 5r, systems 4-5. See Fig. 25]

¹ This upbeat, and the one following in bar 17, are unclear, and the reading uncertain. In each case the transcription follows the example of bar 21, where the turn is clearly legible.
² The F sharp appears as a half note.
³ These two notes seem to be unrelated to the surrounding sketches.

FIG. 23. Wittgenstein Sketchbook fol. 4ʳ

182

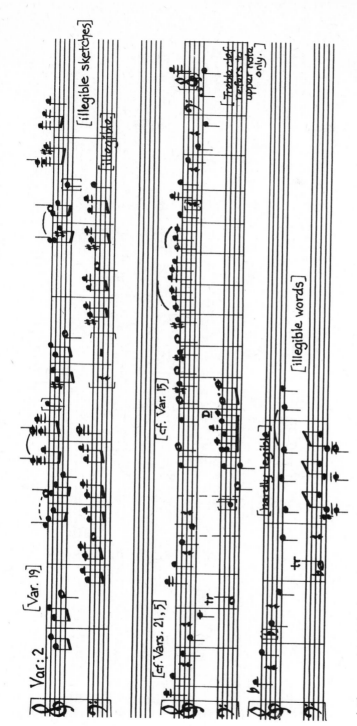

[^1]: The note written is clearly F, although D would be more consistent with the pattern of rising sequences.

183

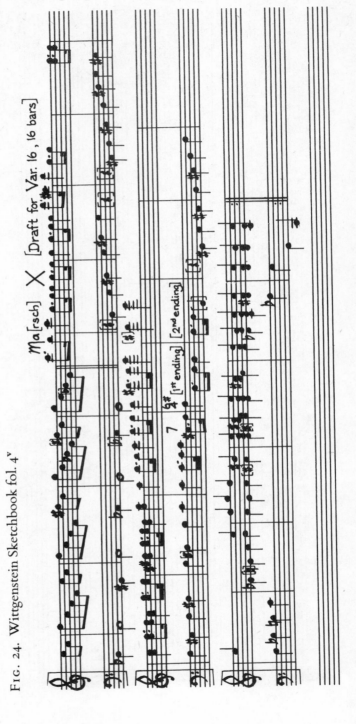

Fig. 24. Wittgenstein Sketchbook fol. 4ᵛ

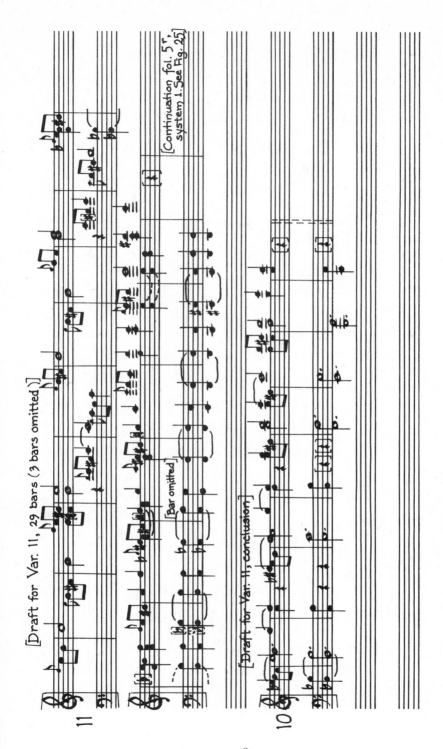

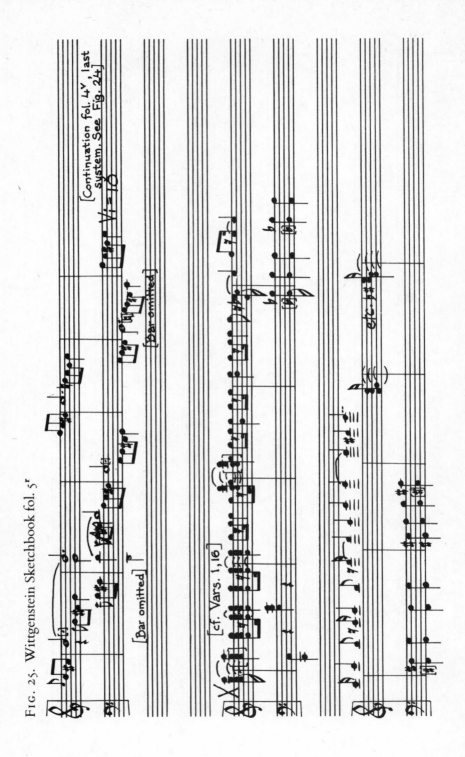

Fig. 25. Wittgenstein Sketchbook fol. 5^r

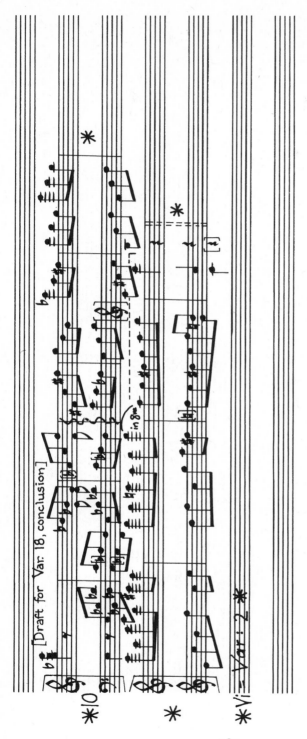

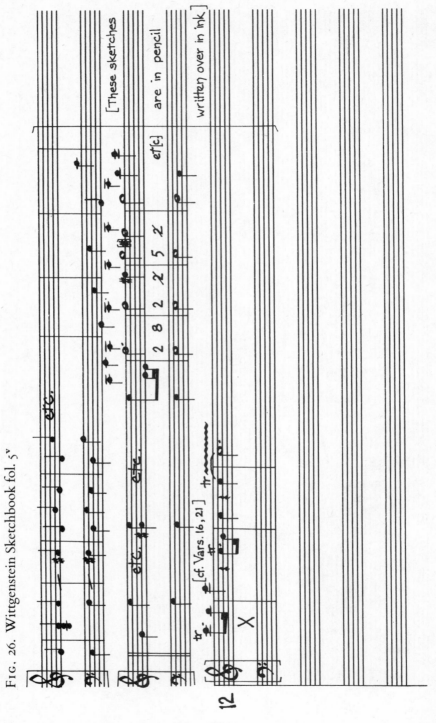

FIG. 26. Wittgenstein Sketchbook fol. 5ᵛ

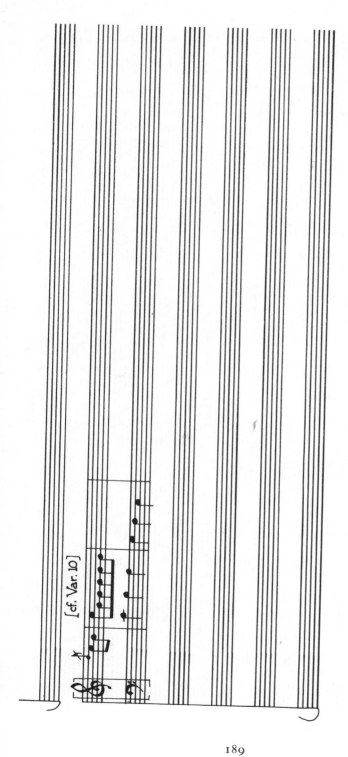

Fig. 27. Wittgenstein Sketchbook fol. 6ʳ

[cf. Var. 5]

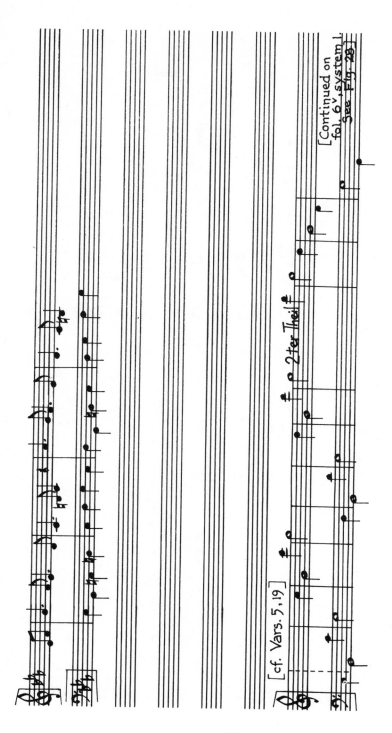

FIG. 28. Wittgenstein Sketchbook fol. 6ᵛ

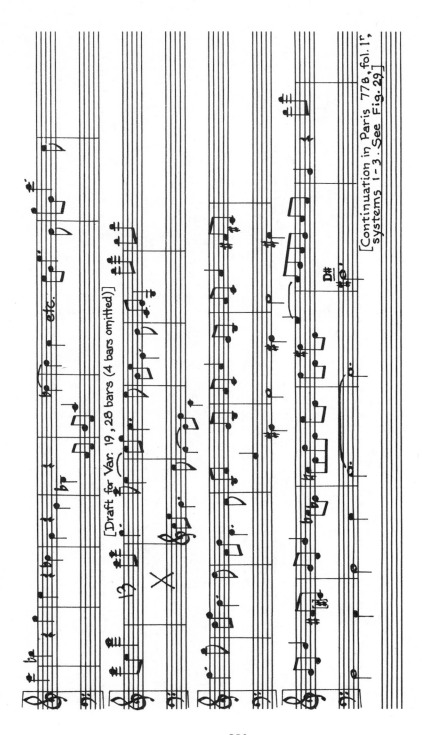

193

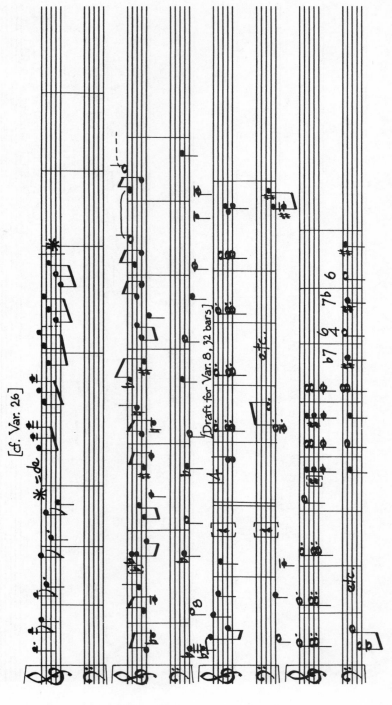

FIG. 29. Paris 77B fol. 1r

[cf. Var. 26]

[Draft for Var. 8, 32 bars]

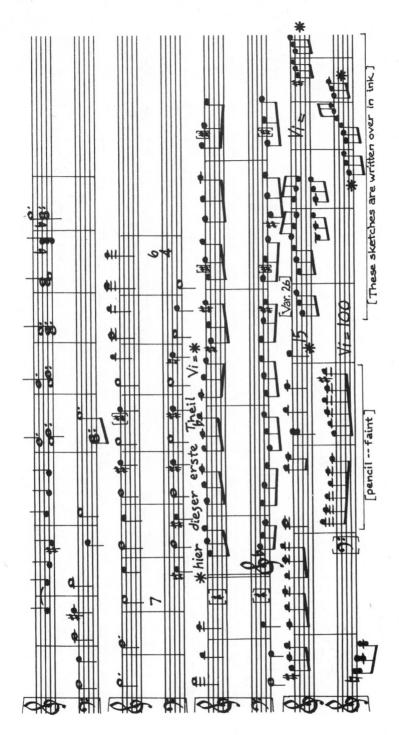

FIG. 30. Paris 77B fol. 1ᵛ

196

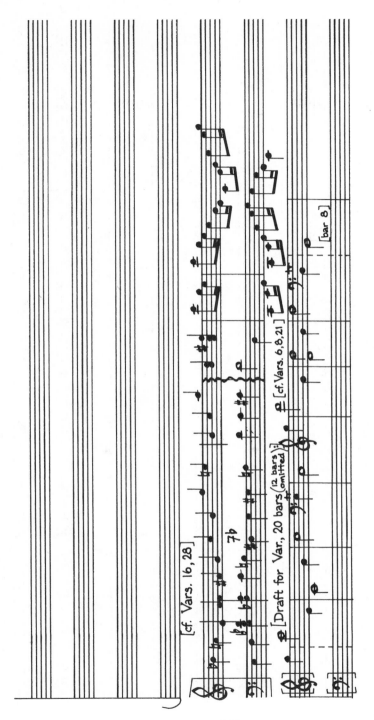

FIG. 31. Paris 77B fol. 2r

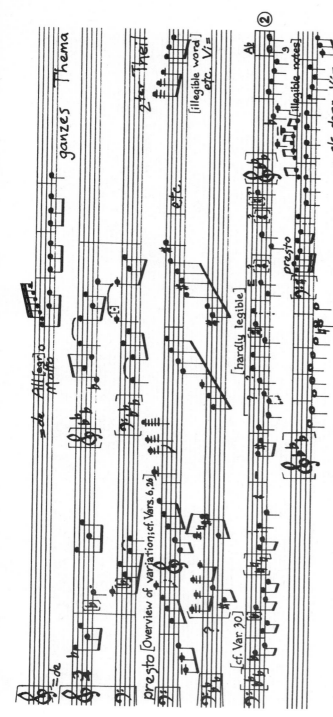

[1] The harmonic progression of this sketch closely resembles the end of the first half of Var. 14, with the progression leading not to E minor, as in the finished variation, but to A minor. Material relating specifically to this variation is conspicuously absent from the Wittgenstein Sketchbook. A variant of this sketch appears on the Autograph Leaf, verso, systems 1–2 (see Fig. 2 and Plate 2).

[2] A seventeenth stave has been provided below to accommodate the continuation of this sketch. In the original MS, the entire sketch is contained on the sixteenth stave.

FIG. 32. Paris 77B fol. 2ᵛ

200

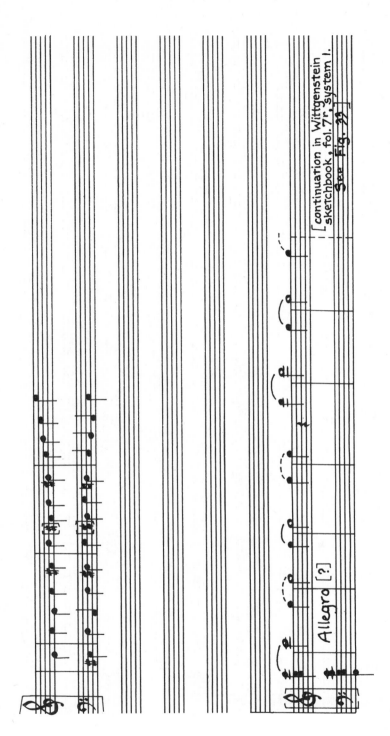

[continuation in Wittgenstein sketchbook, fol.7r, system I. See Fig. 22.]

Allegro [?]

201

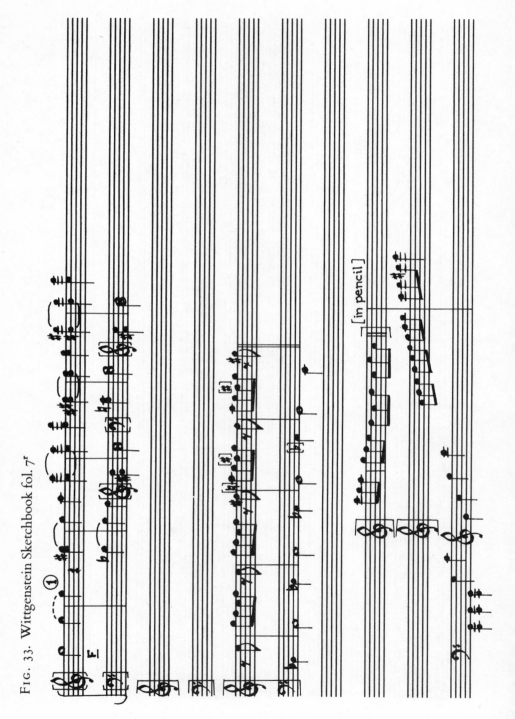

Fɪɢ. 33. Wittgenstein Sketchbook fol. 7ʳ

¹ Cf. Autograph Leaf, verso, systems 2–3 (Fig. 2); Landsberg 10, p. 170, sketch at bottom of page (Fig. 13).

203

FIG. 34. Wittgenstein Sketchbook fol. 7ᵛ

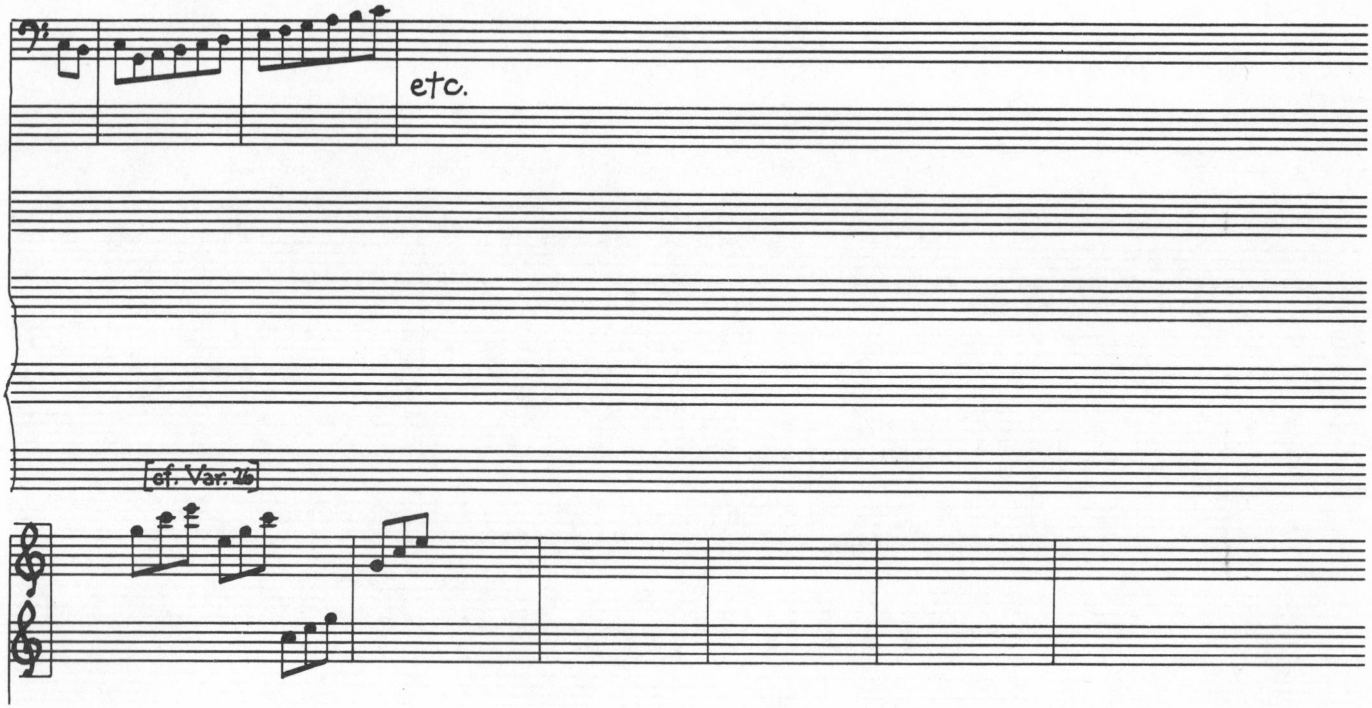

204

205

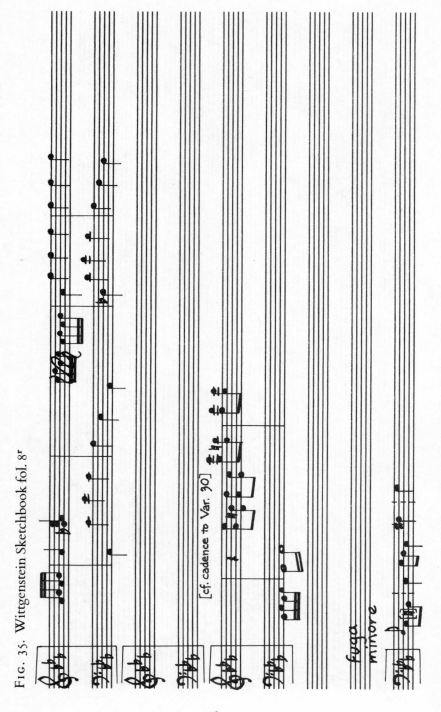

Fig. 35. Wittgenstein Sketchbook fol. 8ʳ

206

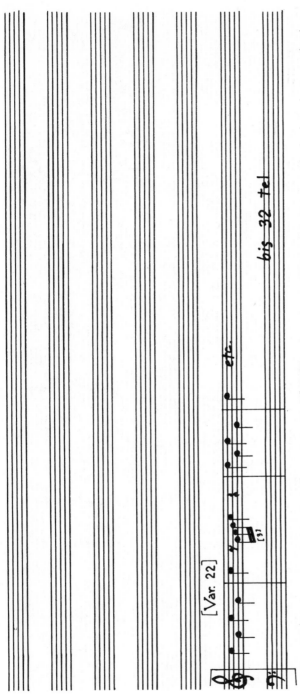

[Var. 22]

bis 32 tel

etc.

[3]

---

[1] This sketch bears a tenuous, and mainly rhythmic, relationship to Diabelli's waltz, and may not belong to the Variations. The sketch may be associated with another entry for a 'Doppelfuge' in the Paris 58 MS, fol. 2r.

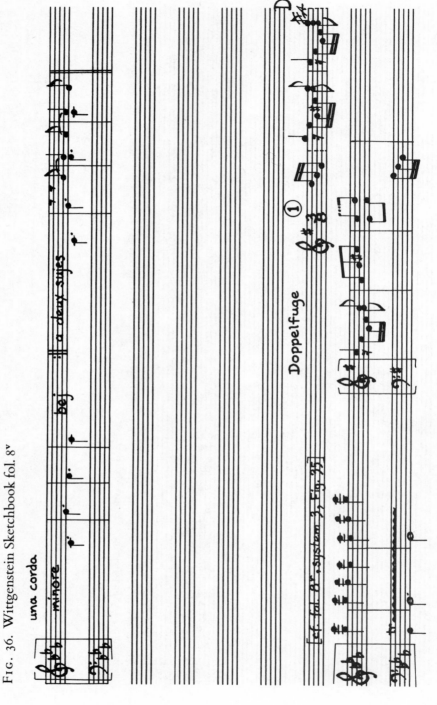

FIG. 36. Wittgenstein Sketchbook fol. 8ᵛ

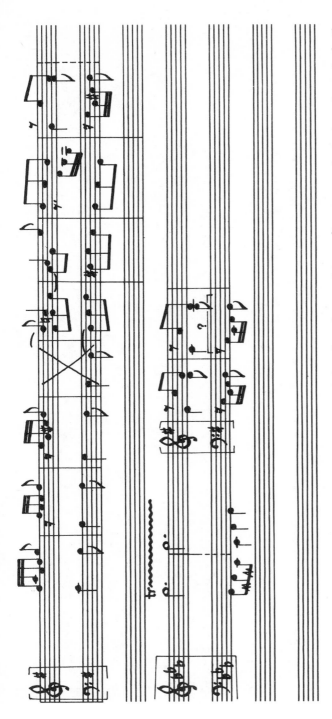

¹ This sketch bears a tenuous, and mainly rhythmic, relationship to Diabelli's waltz, and may not belong to the Variations. The sketch may be associated with another entry for a 'Doppelfuge' in the Paris 58 MS, fol. 2ʳ.

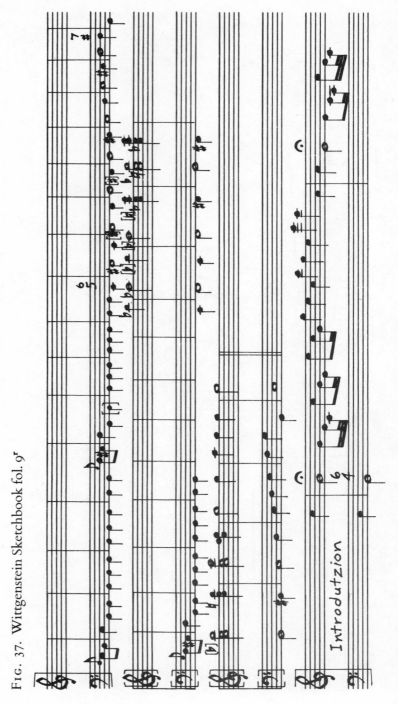

Fig. 37. Wittgenstein Sketchbook fol. 9^r

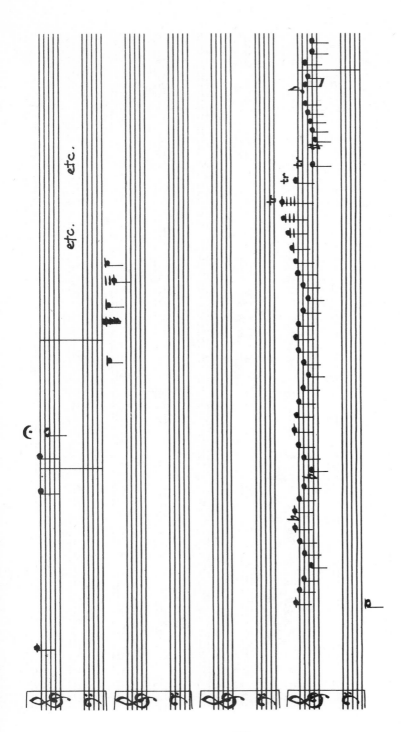

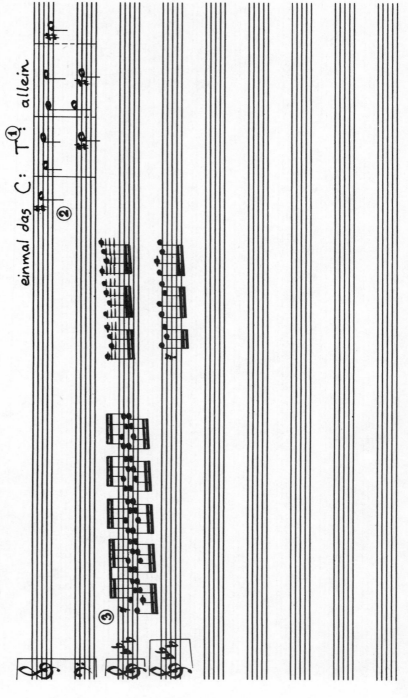

Fig. 38. Wittgenstein Sketchbook fol. 10ᵛ

1 The letters 'C' and 'T' presumably stand for 'C[ontra] T[hema]'. The entire inscription thus reads 'einmal das C[ontra] T[hema] allein'.
2 This sketch may relate to the countersubject of the fugue in half notes; cf. the sketches on the following page, fol. 11r, systems 4–5.
3 These entries probably represent an intensification through rhythmic diminution of the ascending sequence from fol. 11r, systems 2–3.

213

FIG. 39. Wittgenstein Sketchbook fol. 11r

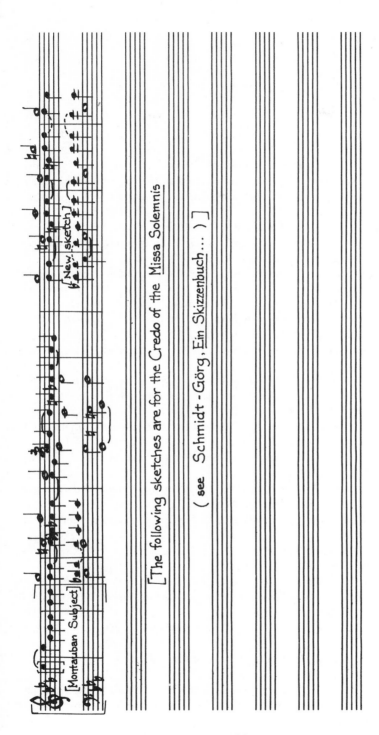

[The following sketches are for the Credo of the Missa Solemnis

(see Schmidt - Görg, Ein Skizzenbuch...)]

215

Bibliography of Works Cited

Abraham, Lars Ulrich: 'Trivialität und Persiflage in Beethovens Diabelli-Variationen', *Neue Wege der musikalischen Analyse* (Veröffentlichungen des Instituts für Neue Musik und Musikerziehung Darmstadt, Vol. 6) (Berlin, 1967), pp. 7–17.

Anderson, Emily: *The Letters of Beethoven*, Vol. III (New York, 1961).

Beethoven, Ludwig van: edition of Op. 120 with commentary by Hans von Bülow (New York, Schirmer, 1926).

— facsimile edition of 'Artaria-Artôt-Trèmont-Engelmann' Sketchbook (*Receuil Thématique/de L. v. Beethoven./Autographe/contenant 37 pages de musique./Donné à Mr. Artôt (célèbre violoniste français)/par Mr. Auguste Artaria, éditeur des ouvrages de/Beethoven, à Vienne le 19 Mai 1835 (Leipzig, 1913)*) (Wilhelm Engelmann Verlag: Leipzig, 1913).

— *Drei Skizzenbücher zur Missa Solemnis*, ed. Joseph Schmidt-Görg (Bonn, 1952–70).

— *Ein Skizzenbuch zu den Diabelli-Variationen und zur Missa Solemnis*, SV 154, ed. Joseph Schmidt-Görg (Bonn, facsimile, 1968; transcription, 1972).

Brandenburg, Sieghard: 'Beethoven's "Erste Entwürfe" zu Variationenzyklen', *Bericht über den Internationalen Musikwissenschaftlichen Kongress, Bonn 1970* (Kassel, 1971), pp. 335–57.

— 'Viewpoint: Beethoven Scholars and Beethoven's Sketches', *19th-Century Music*, ii (1979), pp. 270–4.

— 'Die Skizzen zur Neunten Symphonie', *Zu Beethoven: Aufsätze und Dokumente*, ii, ed. H. Goldschmidt (Berlin, 1984), pp. 88–129.

Butor, Michel: *Dialogue avec 33 variations de Ludwig van Beethoven sur une valse de Diabelli* (Paris, 1971).

Cone, Edward: 'The Late Bagatelles: Beethoven's Experiments in Composition', *Beethoven Studies*, ii, ed. Alan Tyson (London, 1977), pp. 84–105.

Cooper, Martin: *Beethoven: The Last Decade 1817-1827* (London, 1970).

Drabkin, William: *A Study of Beethoven's Opus 111 and its Sources*. Unpublished Ph.D. dissertation (Princeton, 1977).

Geiringer, Karl: 'The Structure of Beethoven's Diabelli Variations', *Musical Quarterly*, l (1964), pp. 496–503.

Goldschmidt, Harry: *Die Erscheinung Beethoven* (Leipzig, 1974).

— *Um die Unsterbliche Geliebte* (Leipzig, 1977).

Gossett, Philip: 'Beethoven's Sixth Symphony: Sketches for the First Movement', *Journal of the American Musicological Society*, xxvii (1974), pp. 248–84.

Halm, August: *Beethoven* (Berlin, 1927).

Johnson, Douglas and Tyson, Alan: 'Reconstructing Beethoven's Sketchbooks', *Journal of the American Musicological Society*, xxv (1972), pp. 137–56.

——, ——, and Winter, Robert: *The Beethoven Sketchbooks: History, Reconstruction, Inventory* (Berkeley and Oxford, 1985).

Kerman, Joseph: *The Beethoven Quartets* (New York, 1967).

Kinderman, William: 'The Evolution and Structure of Beethoven's "Diabelli" Variations', *Journal of the American Musicological Society*, xxxv (1982), pp. 306–28.

—— 'Die Diabelli-Variationen von 1819', *Zu Beethoven: Aufsätze und Dokumente*, ed. H. Goldschmidt (Berlin, 1984), pp. 130–62.

—— 'Beethoven's Symbol for the Deity in the *Missa Solemnis* and the Ninth Symphony', *19th-Century Music*, ix (1985), pp. 102–18.

—— 'Tonality and Form in the Variation Movements of Beethoven's Late Quartets', *Beethoven-Symposion, Bonn 1984* (Bonn, 1987).

Kinsky, Georg and Halm, Hans: *Das Werk Beethovens: Thematisch-bibliographisches Verzeichnis seiner sämtlichen vollendeten Kompositionen* (Munich and Duisburg, 1955).

Kirkendale, Warren: 'New Roads to Old Ideas in Beethoven's Missa Solemnis', *Musical Quarterly*, lvi (1970), pp. 665–701.

Klein, Hans-Günter: *Ludwig van Beethoven, Autographen und Abschriften, Katalog* (Staatsbibliothek preussischer Kulturbesitz, Kataloge der Musikabteilung I, 2) (Berlin, 1975).

Köhler, Karl-Heinz and Beck, Dagmar: eds., *Ludwig van Beethovens Konversationshefte*, 2 (Leipzig, 1976).

Kross, Siegfried: 'Eine problematische Stelle in Beethovens Diabelli-Variationen', *Die Musikforschung*, xvi (1963), pp. 267–70.

—— 'Nochmals zu Beethovens Diabelli-Variationen', *Die Musikforschung*, xviii (1965), pp. 184–5.

Lockwood, Lewis: 'On "Parody" as Term and Concept in 16th-Century Music', *Aspects of Medieval and Renaissance Music: A Birthday Offering to Gustav Reese*, ed. Jan LaRue (New York, 1966), pp. 560–75.

—— 'Beethoven's Unfinished Piano Concerto of 1815: Sources and Problems', *Musical Quarterly*, lvi (1970), pp. 624–46.

—— 'On Beethoven's Sketches and Autographs: Some Problems of Definition and Interpretation', *Acta musicologica*, xiii (1970), pp. 32–47.

Mann, Thomas: *Doctor Faustus. The Life of the German Composer Adrian Leverkühn as Told by a Friend*, trans. by H. T. Lowe-Porter (London, 1949; first published Stockholm, 1947).

Münster, Arnold: *Studien zu Beethovens Diabelli-Variationen* (Munich, 1982).

Nottebohm, Gustav: *Zweite Beethoveniana* (Leipzig, 1887; repr. New York, 1970).

Porter, David: 'The Structure of Beethoven's Diabelli Variations, Op. 120', *Music Review*, xxxi (1970), pp. 295-7.

Reynolds, Christopher: 'Beethoven's Sketches for the Variations in E^b Op. 35', *Beethoven Studies*, iii, ed. Alan Tyson (Cambridge, 1982), pp. 47-84.

Riezler, Walter: *Beethoven* (Berlin and Zürich, 1936).

Rosen, Charles: *The Classical Style* (New York, 1972).

Schindler, Anton: *Beethoven As I Knew Him*, trans. Constance S. Jolly, ed. Donald MacArdle (London and Chapel Hill, 1966).

Schmidt, Hans: 'Verzeichnis der Skizzen Beethovens', *Beethoven-Jahrbuch*, vi, Jg. 1965/68 (1969), pp. 7-128.

Solomon, Maynard: *Beethoven* (New York, 1977).

Thayer, Alexander Wheelock: *Chronologisches Verzeichniss der Werke Ludwig van Beethovens* (Berlin, 1865).

—— *Life of Beethoven*, ed. Elliot Forbes (Princeton, 1964).

Tovey, Donald Francis: *Essays in Musical Analysis: Chamber Music* (London, 1944).

—— *Beethoven* (London, 1945).

Tyson, Alan: 'Weiteres über die problematische Stelle in Beethovens Diabelli-Variationen', *Die Musikforschung*, xviii (1965), pp. 46-8.

—— 'Notes on Five of Beethoven's Copyists', *Journal of the American Musicological Society*, xxiii (1970), pp. 460-3.

—— 'A Reconstruction of the Pastoral Symphony Sketchbook', *Beethoven Studies*, i, ed. Alan Tyson (New York, 1973), pp. 67-96.

—— 'Das Leonore Skizzenbuch (Mendelssohn 15): Probleme der Rekonstruktion und Chronologie', *Beethoven Jahrbuch*, ix, Jg. 1973/77 (1977), pp. 469-500.

Uhde, Jürgen: *Beethovens Klaviermusik*, vol. I (Stuttgart, 1968).

Winter, Robert: Review of *Ludwig van Beethoven: Ein Skizzenbuch zu den Diabelli-Variationen und zur Missa Solemnis*, SV 154, ed. Joseph Schmidt-Görg, in *Journal of the American Musicological Society*, xxviii (1975), pp. 135-8.

—— 'Plans for the Structure of the String Quartet in C sharp Minor, Op. 131', *Beethoven Studies*, ii, ed. Alan Tyson (London, 1977), pp. 106-37.

—— 'The Sketches for the "Ode to Joy" ', in *Beethoven, Performers, and Critics. The International Beethoven Congress, Detroit, 1977*, ed. R. Winter and B. Carr (Detroit, 1980), pp. 176-214.

—— *Compositional Origins of Beethoven's Opus 131* (Ann Arbor, 1982).

Yeomans, William: 'Problems of Beethoven's Diabelli Variations', *Monthly Musical Record*, lxxxix (1959), pp. 8-13.

Zenk, Martin: 'Rezeption von Geschichte in Beethovens "Diabelli-Variationen", Zur Vermittlung analytischer, ästhetischer, und historischer Kategorien', *Archiv für Musikwissenschaft*, xxxvii (1980), pp. 61-75.

Index of Names and Works